D0649787

LEAP

Lifetime Economic Acceleration Process

LEAP

Lifetime Economic Acceleration Process

By Robert Castiglione

CASTLE LION
PUBLISHERS

The Library of Congress has catalogued this book as follows:

Library of Congress Control Number: 2005930876

ISBN 0-9771171-0-3

Printed in Canada

Table of Contents

Acknowledgements

Like any book, this one has been inspired by many people. From family members to professional colleagues, I thank them all for their encouragement and contributions. For over twenty-five years, I have seen hundreds, maybe thousands, of financial books come and go. So many are filled with the same tired information that one day I decided to write the one book that people can use and be supported by their professional financial advisors.

Writing a book is a difficult task, especially looking at the first blank screen in the word processor. You dig down deep and get ideas—some good, some not so good. Some days, you can't get a word out; other days they flow like a river. But most writers will tell you that there are people in their lives that help make it all come together and happen.

My wife, Marilyn, has provided great support for more than thirty years and has been a constant source of motivation and compassion. During the year this book has been in process, she has helped me specifically to carve out time to work on it. As a retired schoolteacher, she would read my work and give me a grade, usually bringing both of us to laughter. But in the end, she was my inspiration to get the work completed.

My two sons, Christian and Craig, have both joined me in business over the past few years since finishing college. They are both insightful and thoughtful about new directions, both for the business and for how to articulate what we do at LEAP Systems. And they have always been willing to let me bounce ideas for the book off them. No father could ask for more from his sons than that which is founded on love and respect.

The LEAP Systems staff has shown an unending endurance for the many hours I kept them to help me get the work processed. Their efforts behind the scenes are a key part of the entire LEAP story. So I want to personally thank Art Sanger, Alison Huchko, Jim Nicoletti, George Signoriello, Heather Kruger, Matt Friebis, Rod Miller, Tara Castiglione, Jill Molitor, Freeman

Dean, and my printer Bill Metcalf for their technical support and the coordinating skills they provide every day to make our operation run smoothly.

Our entire training force use their wonderful ability to get our message out to thousands of LEAP representatives at the highest standards of content knowledge and customer service, both of which I have worked to bring into this manuscript. Stan Kacala has been training for me in three decades, and from our business relationship has come a close friendship. Without Stan at my side, LEAP would not be where it is today. Then there are Art Sanger, Chuck McDowell, Mark Beiting, Ron Johnson, Trent Fortner, and Saul Cohen, our National Trainers who have made LEAP grow over the years into a premier personal-wealth-building organization. There are also the 25 LEAP Ambassadors, who act as "big brothers" to the new LEAP representatives who join us from year to year.

LEAP representatives are the heart and soul of the company. Without them there would be no book. Their love of and dedication to the principles of the LEAP System provide me with the energy I need to continue the effort to bring to the public the information they need to reach financial success. These representatives are the purpose for writing this book. They are the people who bring the LEAP System to the public, so that the public can enjoy their personal financial lives.

My close friend Dan Solin provided me with the spark to write this book. Dan is an expert on securities law and author of a book on securities arbitration. He suggested that I broaden my audience for the LEAP vision by publishing a book. He has provided me with valuable advice about publishing and has helped me sharpen my understanding of the public's wariness about purveyors of financial advice. One of my joys was to be interviewed by Dan on his television show in Florida. I always turned to Dan for advice on writing this book, since he has written three himself.

Finally there are the professionals who worked specifically on this book. Jon Zonderman, a writer who specializes in collaborating with experts on their books, helped to conceptualize the book's structure and worked with me on successive drafts to fine-tune the message. Tommy Dunne did the copy editing and production editing. And Meghan McPhail provided the wonderful designs for both the inside pages and the cover.

So there you have it. It takes the coordination and involvement of many people to complete a book. I learned a great deal during the process, and I hope that you will learn a great deal more from the contents of this book and enjoy the happy and prosperous financial life that you deserve.

Foreword

There is no shortage of information about the subject of personal finance. Indeed, I know of no subject where there is more information and less comprehension. What accounts for this anomaly?

It is not for lack of motivation. Americans are highly motivated to learn everything they can in order to secure their financial futures and the financial well-being of their families. So prevalent is this concern that one major brokerage firm attempts to measure it with an index that reflects investor optimism in the economy.

It is not for lack of spending. The financial industry is a well-oiled marketing machine that spends hundreds of millions of dollars each year advertising its products to an audience eager for information.

It is not for lack of timely information. The financial media has never been more omnipresent. We have twenty-four-hour television and radio programs focused entirely on business and financial news. The print media, both magazines and newspapers, deliver an unending stream of information intended to keep us abreast of the latest news that could impact our financial lives.

How, then, is it possible that the vast majority of Americans are in such financial disarray, despite their hard work and their well-intentioned efforts to avoid this predicament? Each year, personal bankruptcy filings break new records. It is now more likely that people will file for personal bankruptcy than for divorce. Consumer debt (excluding mortgages) exceeds $2 _trillion_. Nearly 45 million people lack _any_ health care insurance, and 12 percent of our citizens live in poverty.

Clearly, whatever financial advice we are listening to is not working. On the other end of the spectrum, the financial-services business is booming. In 2004, that industry generated $227 _billion_ in revenue and an estimated $19 _billion_ in profits.

Why the large disparity? As Bob Castiglione explains in this ground-breaking book, traditional financial advice isn't working and a new paradigm is needed. He clearly points out why and how his dynamic financial model—Lifetime Economic Acceleration Process—works. It is so logical that one must contemplate how current financial theory and advice even got started. It is in your best interest to maintain control of your personal income and assets and to multiply the tremendous benefits you can derive from them.

Unfortunately, achieving financial success means being able to discard what have become almost sacred beliefs. After reading this book, I walked away thinking that most of the other so-called financial experts are driven by their own self-interest, and not the public's. It is not surprising that, when these "experts" try to educate the rest of us, their efforts merely serve to perpetuate more misinformation and confusion. There are almost too many of these sacred beliefs to count.

There are few financial "experts" with the insight, knowledge, and courage to challenge these beliefs. Bob Castiglione is one such financial visionary. The holistic principles of sound personal financial advice he sets forth in this book are clear and easy to follow, and are based on irrefutable principles of economics and finance. They would stand the test of any honest and rational analysis.

Bob's explanations about how we should view and use money will change the way all of us think about how to accumulate wealth. It takes someone as extraordinary as Bob to set the record straight and debunk the myths of what now passes for financial planning. I have equal respect for your judgment in choosing to take this LEAP to financial success.

You will be well rewarded for your efforts.

Daniel R. Solin
Bonita Springs, Florida

Daniel R. Solin is a securities arbitration attorney, a
registered investment advisor and the author of
Does Your Broker Owe You Money? *(Silvercloud, 2004).*

Author's Preface

As a young boy, I worked many odd jobs. I cut lawns, shoveled snow, delivered milk door-to-door, and worked in a supermarket. My dad taught me to save my money and matched every dollar I put into the bank. Seeing my account grow was a great incentive and a wonderful lesson at an early age about the importance of savings.

Most of my childhood was dedicated to school and sports. I excelled at baseball and dreamed of becoming a major-league baseball player. The day I graduated from high school I was offered a baseball contract by the San Francisco Giants. My dad and I discussed it and we decided that I should go to college instead. I used my savings to pay for part of my education—this was one of the great lessons in life that I still cherish today.

At New York University's School of Business and Finance, I studied accounting, marketing, management, economics, and finance. I proudly graduated with a bachelor of science degree in economics. I had maintained my interest and talent in baseball and was eventually drafted by the Minnesota Twins. I signed a bonus contract, and off I went to follow my dream.

While many other "bonus baby" baseball players bought cars and other expensive goodies with their signing bonuses, I invested mine for my future, to expand my options for life after baseball—whatever and whenever that would be. In the team clubhouse, I scanned the financial pages of the newspapers ahead of the sports pages, a trait my teammates noted with some amusement. But over time, some players asked me to help them better understand the world of personal finance. I enjoyed providing them with this knowledge, and many appreciated their newfound financial success.

While other players worked odd jobs in the off-season, I went to Wall Street and obtained my licenses in the financial services business. Not only was I having a successful baseball career, but I had a large clientele from my financial practice in the off-season as well. After spending five years in professional baseball and obtaining a major-league contract, I suffered a ruptured appendix, and that led to other serious medical complications.

I decided to trade in my childhood dream of being a major-league baseball player for a new dream of becoming a success in the financial services industry. I applied the same habits I learned as a professional athlete to develop into a major-league financial advisor—knowledge, skill, dedication, and focus.

Although knowledge of a subject is vital to participate in any profession, it will not necessarily lead to success, unless you combine it with skill, dedication, and focus. It's the difference between teaching art history and creating art, or being a great golf coach and being able to compete under tournament pressure as a professional tour player. Very few athletes or artists reach the pinnacle of their profession without being single-minded in their effort to achieve success.

Over the years, I have observed that most people have little knowledge or skill in handling their own money. They are too busy at their own job, making money for their employer or running their own business, and bringing home a paycheck to make ends meet for themselves and their families. But that's where it ends. Few people are successful at making their savings and investments work efficiently and effectively, and many are actually preventing themselves from enjoying their income and obtaining financial well-being.

The game of personal finance is a difficult one to master. If dedication and focus are missing, there is little chance of attaining personal financial success. In this book, I will provide you with the financial education and skill, but you will need to supply the dedication and focus to improve your financial life. If you want to get to the big leagues in personal finance, it is going to take knowledge, skill, dedication, and focus.

In the nearly forty years I have been teaching personal finance and economics, I have advised professional athletes, executives of Fortune 500 companies, partners at top accounting firms, lawyers, and people from all walks of life. Over twenty-five of the largest financial institutions in North America have used my systems, knowledge, and know-how to improve their financial services operations, to add value for their clients, and to build a better image for themselves.

By using the information in this book, you will be more knowledgeable and better able to use, grow, and protect your money in a more efficient and effective manner. Anyone can do it, without taking big risks, without a large investment, and with the right mixture of knowledge, skill, dedication and focus. You will be empowered with money concepts that will make the difference in your life and that of your family and future heirs.

Robert Castiglione
Bridgewater, New Jersey
July 2005

Introduction

Understanding money—how it works, how to grow it, and how to protect it from the vicissitudes of taxes, market fluctuation, suit, inflation, expenses, and other eroding factors—has been my life's work. Over the years I have developed a personal financial process to build and protect wealth in the most effective and efficient manner. It is called the Lifetime Economic Acceleration Process (LEAP).

The main principle behind the LEAP system is that money should perform in a "multiplier" fashion rather than acting only once, as when it is accumulating or compounding in most financial products.

When money accumulates, it works basically like this:

$4 today + another $4 tomorrow = $8

What if money could work in this manner?

$4 today x another $4 tomorrow = $16

Which of the above formulas would you choose to have your money working for you?

Notice that the only difference in these two equations is the symbol that denotes the mathematical operation. The "plus" symbol denotes a world where your wealth grows arithmetically, by accumulation. The "times" symbol in the second formula denotes a world where your wealth grows in a multiplier fashion. We should all want to have our money growing in a multiplier fashion rather than arithmetically. Then why do so many people have their money compounding or accumulating in financial accounts? They should seek methods and strategies that multiply the return and create larger benefits.

Most financial advisors today use only the accumulation-of-money theory rather than working with the multiplier approach. In this book you will learn why the accumulation method is used and why the multiplier methods are not explained or provided to the public. Although using the accumulation process alone can lead to an increase in your assets over time, that increase will fall far short of your money's full financial potential without the use of the multiplier approach. Those who use the accumulation approach alone may never know how much money they are potentially losing.

The LEAP system allows you to use the multiplier effect on your money by coordinating the most advantageous aspects of various financial instruments and integrating them into a cohesive mix of powerful wealth-building financial "strategies."

It is important to your financial well-being to work with a financial advisor who focuses on the principles of obtaining multiplier effects rather than one who only focuses on the accumulation-of-money method. You work too hard for your money, and it is not fair for your money not to work hard for you.

Money in Motion

Newton's Third Law of Physics states that objects at rest tend to stay at rest and objects in motion tend to stay in motion. The same is true for money. Money that is only accumulating in one product is, in essence, at rest. It is only doing one job: accumulating. It is not really doing all it can do for you. It becomes an easy target for the financial eroding factors of taxes, inflation, planned obsolescence, technological change, market fluctuation, interest-rate changes, and more to deplete its value over time.

In contrast, money that is in motion and obtaining a multiplier effect tends to be moving faster than the eroding factors, allowing you to build and protect your wealth better. For money to perform to its fullest potential, it must be set in motion in a well-choreographed manner. A simple analogy I like to use with my clients to illustrate this motion-of-money concept and its multiplier effects is that of a banking institution.

Let's say you deposit $10,000 in a bank account and that bank gives you 5 percent annual interest on your money. How does the bank make money?

The typical answer is that the bank lends your money out to someone else at a higher rate of interest than it provides you, say 9 percent. This 4 percent difference is called the "spread." If that 4 percent spread were all that the bank made, banks would go out of business very quickly. There is simply no way banks could pay their overhead and earn a profit on only a 4 percent spread.

In reality, banks earn at least five times the spread by using money over and over again. This is called the "velocity of money." For example, your $10,000, on which you are earning 5 percent, gets lent out first as a car loan at 9 percent interest. The car dealer then deposits this money back into the banking system. The bank then has the opportunity to lend the same money out a second time, say for a college loan, at 8 percent. The college deposits the money back into the bank.

The bank then lends the money out a third time, this time on a credit card, with a 12 percent interest rate. Again, the merchant deposits the money from the purchases back into the bank. The bank then lends the money out for a fourth time, say for a home mortgage loan, at 6 percent. The home seller deposits the money and the bank lends the money out yet again, for a fifth time, for a home improvement loan, at 8 percent.

At the end of this economic cycle, the bank has earned between 30 and 40 percent in total interest (after paying you only 5 percent) on the $10,000 you deposited. This multiplier use of money enables the bank to earn enough revenue to maintain its headquarters, staff, information technology spending, and have some left over to pay dividends and have an appreciating stock price.

Now, as an individual, you don't have the same capacity or license to loan money that a bank does. And I must tell you that in no way am I suggesting through this bank example that the key to building wealth is to borrow money and have highly leveraged investments. This technique has been suggested by others, and believe me, it is a recipe for potential financial disaster for almost everyone who tries it.

But it is possible for you to derive a multiplier effect on your assets in other secure ways that are safe and reliable. Some are guaranteed by financial institutions and/or the government. The techniques are easy to implement if you follow the LEAP process.

Knowledge, Skill, Dedication, and Focus

In the marketplace today, typically what you see are financial advisors who suggest allocating money to meet future needs and expenses, such as the purchase of a first house, paying for a child's college education, or retirement. All of these allocations, and the accumulation of money toward them, are targeted toward meeting the specific future expense, but many will fall far short of the target and not help people to build real wealth or achieve their full financial potential.

By applying dedication and focus to your financial life and by participating with the knowledge and skill that the LEAP system brings, you can enhance your ability to build and protect your wealth beyond your own expectations.

You should think about working with your money the way NASA works with a space flight. NASA engineers do not let a rocket take off with just enough power to lift it into space, or with just enough fuel to get the astronauts to the moon and back. NASA uses the best materials, plans for many contingencies, and builds in backup plans known as "redundancies."

Every flight has extra fuel, extra rocket thrust, many backup computer systems, and a full team of engineers—not just one—supporting it. Even with all of that, the astronauts themselves provide a great deal of human knowledge and experience to make the mission a success.

Unfortunately, many consumers have financial plans that will not work and will not perform as designed. They don't have enough fuel—money being put into the plan. They do not have enough thrust—financial products that do not perform well in and of themselves. And they don't have backup systems in case something goes wrong—increased taxes, disability, death, inflation, etc. Their plans are not well designed for success if anything goes the slightest bit off course.

For a more sure-footed approach to building and protecting your wealth, you need to treat your financial life like NASA treats every space mission. You need to give your money full thrust, power, protection, redundancy, backup expertise, human knowledge, scientific calculations, and above all else the passion to succeed. This is the essence and philosophy of LEAP.

A Road Map for Action

This book is a road map to achieving your financial well-being and financial success. The reason I wrote this book is to provide you with the truth about money, financial products, and financial strategies, and to reveal any misinformation that often appears in the media, textbooks, and advertising in some parts of the financial services industry. In striving to achieve a healthier financial life, you must incorporate the principles laid out in this book into your everyday thinking and actions.

Chapters 1 through 3 lay out the theories behind personal financial economics and explain how the eroding factors and misinformation hamper your wealth-building efforts. Chapter 4 describes in concise detail the winning strategy using the Lifetime Economic Acceleration Process.

Chapters 5 through 11 discuss seven specific areas of personal economics and why people make inappropriate decisions in regard to such areas of finance as compounding, taxable investments, casualty insurance, life insurance, estate planning, college funding, retirement savings, and real estate/mortgages. In each of these chapters, I explain how the "conventional wisdom" on using financial products is often so wrong and why it is necessary to learn the multiplier approach.

Finally, chapter 12 lays out in greater detail the proper "Road to Travel" when it comes to building and protecting your wealth, living life to its fullest, enjoying your assets, and eventually creating a legacy to pass on for your heirs or your favorite charities.

Much of what you read in this book might seem counterintuitive, because it is not what you have heard before about how to save and invest your money. Since it can be proven that most people are not wealthy, and many live day to day, while some struggle to make ends meet, it is evidence enough that the information they are receiving from traditional sources is not working. Yet the LEAP system has worked for millions of clients of the more than 5,000 LEAP representatives across the United States and Canada. You work hard for your money; now is the time to let your money work hard for you. I have built this system for you to use and enjoy throughout your life. I want to end this introduction with one of my favorite proverbs: "The secret of getting ahead is getting started."

CHAPTER 1

Economic Acceleration: A New Way of Thinking

By reading this book, you will learn why and how your money will be eroded, confiscated, and transferred away—in most cases without you even knowing it. In your lifetime, you will be bombarded with misinformation from the media, from financial books and magazines, and from financial advisors. These forces at work in the financial world are so powerful that you may have little chance to reach your full financial potential.

Your journey through this book will be one of amazement. You will be shown clearly what you need to do in order to avoid the numerous financial pitfalls that await you, and how you can grow and protect your money over time if you understand and use the principles of the Lifetime Economic Acceleration Process (LEAP).

Let's begin the journey by first identifying the three major institutions that influence your financial life. They are:

- **Financial institutions**
- **Government**
- **Corporations**

You must know and understand how these institutions affect your life and every financial decision you make. Without this knowledge, you may be unable to take advantage of the financial opportunities, products, and strategies that can make your financial life more enjoyable—and help you become financially successful.

Financial Institutions

Financial institutions are the companies that build financial products intended to protect, store, or grow your money. These financial institutions are the engines of our capitalist system. Without banks, insurance companies, investment companies, stock brokerages, real estate firms, and the financial markets, our civilization would be far less vibrant than it is today. I would not want to live in any nation without these financial institutions.

Keep in mind, however, that these financial institutions are profit-making businesses. While supplying their customers with financial products and services, they most certainly make profits for their executives, managers, employees, and shareholders. You must always keep in mind that they are only a conduit between you and your money. They make their money by accumulating, lending, and investing their customers' money and charging fees, commissions, or interest.

Financial institutions also employ many intelligent, creative, and highly skilled people who develop ways to improve their business interests. Consumers, on the other hand, are not generally experts in financial matters. They have not been specifically trained or educated in personal financial matters. Most consumers are too busy trying to earn a living and lack the time to learn how to make their money work for them. Consumers choose to give their money to financial institutions to care for it, watch it, and, they hope, "grow" it.

Financial institutions have a clear advantage over consumers in knowing how to use money to build their wealth. Many consumers, on the other hand, never get to build real wealth or reach their full financial potential. This book will show you how to interact with financial institutions in order to improve your ability to build and protect your wealth.

Government

The government's impact on your financial life is enormous. Government entities at the federal, state, and local levels regulate the money supply, make financial laws, collect income and other taxes, and provide financial and social services.

The government complicates your financial life because it keeps changing the rules and laws that affect your ability to keep and grow your money. Although federal income taxes are the most serious wealth-eroding factor you face, other forms of taxation also affect your financial well-being—everything from gasoline taxes to cigarette and other excise taxes, Social Security taxes, sales taxes, unemployment taxes, state income taxes, property taxes, and estate taxes. When all forms of taxation are considered, many people are in a very high tax bracket—meaning taxes as a percentage of income—without even knowing it. This book will show you ways to lower your taxes without difficulty, risk, or added cost.

Corporations

Corporations make the consumer products and design the services we all need and want in order to live our lives. The number of products and services available to us is almost infinite, and ever changing. Corporations are also extremely savvy in knowing how to get at our money over and over again. Products become obsolete, break down, and need to be replaced. Styles change, creating a demand for "new and improved" products. The amount of money paid by consumers to acquire products and services has a direct effect on their ability to grow substantial wealth. This book will provide information on how to have your money work over and over again, making it more efficient and effective for everyday use, while still leaving plenty of money for wealth building and retirement income.

Financial Tools and Controls

The three major financial influences in your life—financial institutions, government, and corporations—have all the tools and ability to control and affect your financial well-being. They use interest charges, fees, commissions, market fluctuation, taxes, inflation, planned obsolescence, technological change, style changes, and a host of other factors that can diminish your personal money supply.

How many financial tools or controls to defend against these eroding factors do you have? The financial game of life is so one-sided that your chances of building wealth become very slim. The vast majority of people in North America will never grow wealth and will experience many financial problems throughout their lifetime. They will lose more money than they will be able to build up or keep.

When I began my career in the financial services industry and studied the economic statistics on how many people fail to build wealth, I was shocked. When I questioned financial advisors about it, the answer I received most often was: "People don't plan to fail, they simply fail to plan."

Something about that reasoning really bothered me. I rejected the notion that if people really wanted to avoid financial failure, as most people do, all they had to do was simply plan. **After years of delving into the matter, I discovered the real reason people fail to achieve wealth: People are planning, but they are planning all wrong.**

It is true that people don't deliberately plan to fail. But it is not true that people who plan will necessarily succeed. The truth is that most people's financial plans are not built for financial success. Many financial advisors say that all you have to do is set aside money each and every year for a variety of future needs and goals. Unfortunately, this is not all there is to it. **Even if you do save systematically, don't spend it, and get a high rate of return, you still may not have a chance to acquire wealth. The eroding factors in our world will take your money away faster than you can build it if you are not prepared to defend your money from such confiscation.**

That is why I have spent essentially my entire adult life looking for an effective and efficient way to build and protect individual wealth for consumers. After many years of research and development, I came up with the ideal method, which I call the Lifetime Economic Acceleration Process (LEAP). This process enables you to work skillfully with financial institutions, government, and corporations to better build and protect your wealth. LEAP helps you build wealth and provides a means of protecting your money against the eroding factors that can destroy your money before you ever get to enjoy it. If you follow the LEAP rules, you can begin to build defenses against the eroding factors that will confront you and your money throughout your lifetime.

Avoiding the Financial Pitfalls

The first and most important step in building financial wealth and happiness is to understand the financial traps and pitfalls that are all around you. Some are obvious while others are not. The ones that are not obvious often have the most devastating effect on your wealth-building potential. These hidden pitfalls don't get explained by many financial advisors. Once you have these eroding factors explained to you and understand their destructive effect on your money, you will be amazed at how easy it is to find ways to avoid them.

In order to participate successfully in the financial world, you must establish and employ defenses and countermeasures that protect your money under any set of circumstances. In other words: **A financial plan that does not work under every set of circumstances is no plan at all.**

Anyone can design a financial plan that can work under the best set of circumstances. But will the plan work for you under a specific set of economic or financial circumstances? What if interest rates drop, the market declines, taxes go up, inflation increases, you get sued, you become disabled, you need more income, you can't get at your money because government changed the rules, your investment portfolio did not perform as well as you thought it would, or any other unforeseen financial disaster occurs? Most financial planning today is not designed to handle any of these circumstances. A sound financial plan should work under any scenario.

Why aren't financial plans designed to help consumers reach their full financial potential and help defend against the eroding factors? Most financial advisors are well meaning. They are trained to provide financial advice and help consumers reach their financial needs and objectives. But the tools and education they have received fall short of providing a solid foundation of planning technology that will work under any set of circumstances. Too much emphasis is placed on offensive strategies and not enough on defensive ones. Their plans are vulnerable to all sorts of changes in economic, market, and taxation conditions.

As a consumer, you need to be aware of the forces at work within our society that make your job of providing financial security for you and your family more difficult. **As in any sporting event, you must know your opposition in order to have any chance of winning the game.** Yet you treat the opposition with respect and sportsmanship, win or lose. The financial institutions, government, and corporations may be viewed as the opposition, but they are not your enemies. We need them in order to have happy and successful lives. But we must know how to work with them effectively to achieve the results we desire. The following section will give you important insights on how to work with financial institutions.

THE FOUR BASIC RULES OF FINANCIAL INSTITUTIONS

Imagine for a moment that you are the president of a financial institution, whether it is a bank, insurance company, brokerage firm, bond house, or mutual fund. What rules and principles would you instill in your employees in order to make your financial institution profitable and successful? My years of research and interviews have revealed an amazing set of facts; the strategy of financial institutions can be stated in four basic rules.

I want to share those four rules with you. Again, I want you to imagine yourself as the president of a financial institution as I ask you the following questions, each of which corresponds to one of the four basic rules:

1. As president, do you want consumers to give your institution their money?

Yes, of course you do. Not only do you want consumers to give you money, you want them to give you as much money as possible. That's because the more money you are able to receive from consumers, the more money you have to put to work and the more profit you can potentially make.

FIRST RULE: Financial institutions want and need your money.

2. As president, do you want consumers to give you their money systematically?

Yes, most certainly you want that as well. If consumers give you money on a regular basis, you have a steady stream of money to put to work for the company. Since you have overhead on a monthly basis, you need a steady income to manage the company well. And, if you have consumers giving you money systematically, it costs you less in marketing and advertising costs to obtain more money.

SECOND RULE: Financial institutions want your money systematically and on an ongoing basis.

3. As president, do you want to hold on to the money consumers give you for a long period of time?

Yes, emphatically. The longer you hold their money, the more money your company makes. Your fees, charges, and investment returns will be more substantial.

THIRD RULE: Financial institutions want to hold your money for as long as possible.

4. As president, How much of consumers' money do you want to give back to them when they ask for it?

The answer might be as little as possible. This is similar to the third rule. Since you make more money holding on to people's money, it also pays for you not to give them too much money when they want it back. However, this must be done in a way that adheres to your contractual obligations and to all applicable laws and regulations.

FOURTH RULE: Financial institutions want to give back as little money as possible.

These are the general objectives of financial institutions because these four rules provide them with the ability to make more of a profit. You should agree that these would be the rules you would set up if you were the president of any financial institution.

Since profitability is their primary objective, financial institutions develop financial products and services that follow the four rules. Not only do they build their products and services to meet these four rules, but they use government to help establish new laws that support their objectives.

Let it be known that I too would follow these rules and objectives if I were president of a financial institution. It is not wrong for them to seek these objectives. It is their capitalist right, and all of us should support their freedom to do so. However, we do not have to relinquish our right to have our money working most efficiently and effectively for us too. We should have rules that meet our objectives and provide us with greater control of our financial capabilities.

Changing the Rules

If you agree that what is best for a financial institution may not always be best for you as well, you are on the right track. But keep in mind that I am not proposing the idea that financial institutions are to be avoided. As a matter of fact, they build the financial tools that provide the financial security we need.

How do you as a consumer establish your own financial rules that help build and protect your wealth? You must learn, with the help of this book, to use financial products in the way most advantageous to you with the least amount of risk and erosion. **You must develop strategies that give you more control, have your money working more efficiently, enable you to pay less income taxes, give you more flexibility to meet changing conditions, and have less risk.**

The relationship between you and financial institutions is one of the keys to wealth building and sound financial security. An analogy I like to use to help you understand this relationship is that of building a house. A lumberyard manufactures and supplies many products you need to build a home. But you probably would not go to a lumberyard and ask the folks there to design and build your home. You would prefer to have architects, engineers, and home-building companies do that job.

In building your financial home, you should be just as careful not to use the financial lumberyard as the designer of your plan. You need their products to build your financial home, but you need financial architects who know how to get the most out of those products and use them in the ways most beneficial to you. If you think of financial institutions as lumberyards, you will have a better understanding of how to work with them and with your money. You need a person who can create strategies to use the financial products that allow your money to work more efficiently and effectively for you.

In this book, I am promoting the idea that you need financial architects—people who can listen to your desires and aspirations as well as understand your needs; people who will work within your budget, bring expertise and skill to the table, and have you participate in the entire process. **A financial architect can help you select the products from the financial institutions and provide you with the knowledge you need to enhance each product's advantages while eliminating or minimizing its disadvantages.** You will also want a financial architect versed in LEAP.

Many financial planners and advisors use a boilerplate financial plan into which they simply plug in your personal financial numbers and then perform a set of calculations to quantify your needs and goals and determine your deficiencies. They then ask you to put more money into their products to satisfy these deficiencies. The plan is essentially the same for everyone. Only the numbers are different. Such plans contain the products and strategies that may help accomplish the four rules of financial institutions, but they're not designed to maximize your financial potential.

On the other hand, **LEAP uses cost-effective and efficient strategies and products that are designed to help your money have a multiplier effect that may result in more money supply and wealth-protection benefits.** We will continue to discuss these differences throughout this book.

Most consumers make the mistake of asking their financial advisors,

"What product should I invest my money in?" or "Where should I put my money?" They mean well, but these are actually the wrong questions to ask. These are lumberyard questions and not ones that you would ask an architect. Rather, you should ask, "How should I save and invest my money?" This question acknowledges that the answer to building and protecting wealth does not lie in the specific financial products you buy, but in how you use the various financial products in combination with each other.

Another analogy I use with my clients and students to get them to understand this important concept is the golf swing. The key to improving your golf game does not lie in buying the latest set of golf clubs. Improving your golf game lies in three areas:

- **Improving your swing**
- **Improving the way you "manage" the course**
- **Improving the way you recover from unforced errors**

As in golf, so too do these rules apply to your personal financial life. I like to emphasize that you need to learn how to properly "swing" your money, how to properly manage the use of financial products, and how to recover from prior financial mismanagement and misinformation.

In each chapter of this book, I will add a key aspect of the LEAP model that will help you develop an understanding to move forward to a position where you may build and protect your wealth more efficiently and effectively.

KEY POINTS
- **Financial institutions, government, and corporations influence your financial life.**
- **A sound financial plan must work under any set of circumstances.**
- **It is not where you put your money but how you use it that matters most.**

CHAPTER 2

Eroding Factors

Just as the laws of physics say that an object at rest will tend to stay at rest and erode over time, if money stays at rest, it too will erode over time. Many financial advisors, as well as most members of the public, do not understand the natural laws of money or how money actually works.

Many people believe they can create a successful financial plan by simply using mathematical calculations to meet their stated future needs and goals. First, they calculate how much money will be needed in the future. Second, they subtract what they already have. Third, they plug in a rate of return by assessing their risk tolerance, and fourth, they calculate how much money they need to put into the plan annually to make up for the deficiency. Often I see clients who have such a financial plan designed for their children's college education or their own retirement. Although the plan may look good, wrapped in a glossy cover with many bar or pie charts inside, the novice eye will not be able to see the flaws or understand why the plan in all likelihood cannot work.

Let's explore the reasons why such financial planning will probably not hold up over time, and why using such a plan may cause you to not meet or satisfy your real financial needs, goals, and desires.

The most obvious fallacy of most financial planning today, yet one that is often overlooked by consumers, is the impossibility in the long run to keep constant the mathematical assumptions used in the calculations. These mathematical assumptions include interest rates, investment returns, tax rates, and inflation rates. These assumptions are certain to change and wreak havoc on the plan. Even if one were to conduct regular reviews of the plan to make adjustments to these assumptions, time may not allow the plan to get back on course. For instance, if stock-market declines or income-tax-rate increases take money away from your plan, it may take many years to recover—or worse, you may be required to put more money into the plan.

Why do so many well-meaning financial advisors develop financial plans for their clients that have a high probability of failure? It is because they lack the knowledge and education to know how to create and build successful plans.

Another fallacy of financial planning is the belief that mathematics is the only function needed in the plan design. Financial advisors utilize numbers and mathematics to develop plans, as if mathematics were all that was necessary. How many times have you heard someone say, "Show me the numbers"? These souls do not understand the natural laws of money.

Let me explain. In mathematics, 4 + 4 = 8. The answer will always be 8, because mathematics is a pure science. We can study math with the certainty that outcomes will always be the same. If I use a handheld calculator or a computer and I input 4 + 4, the calculator or computer will show me the answer, and it will be 8 every time.

This mathematical simplicity does not hold true with money. In other words, if you have $4 today and you need $8 in the future, you cannot simply add $4 and expect the same outcome each time. In mathematics, 8 will be the correct answer, but when dealing with money, it simply is not true. Let's see why.

"Money Is Not Math, and Math Is Not Money"

If there is one key concept to this entire book, and if you take away nothing else from reading it, I hope it would be this: *Money is not math, and math is not money.*

Money is a commodity. It changes in value and can erode over time. This revelation, once you accept it, will increase your chance of having long-lasting financial success. If you think money acts like math, as many financial advisors do, you will always be vulnerable, and chances are that you will not succeed.

Let me give you an example of what I mean when I say that money is a commodity. Suppose you have four oranges on your kitchen table, and you go to the store and buy four more oranges and bring them home and place them on the kitchen table. How many oranges will you now have on the kitchen table? If you say eight oranges, you are right, because you used a mathematical calculation to solve this arithmetic problem.

But what if you left the oranges on the kitchen table, and never ate them, for twenty years. How many oranges would you have left on the kitchen table twenty years from today? Of course, the correct answer would be none. Why would that be?

Mathematically, you should still have eight oranges, but in reality there are none. That's because the oranges would disintegrate or erode over the twenty years. Oranges are not like math, and math is not like an orange. An orange is a commodity. It has physical properties. You need to know about chemistry and its effects on oranges in order to predict how many oranges there will be in the future. You need to know that oranges erode or deteriorate over time. Or someone may even eat one or more of the oranges before the twenty years are up. You can't eat math.

The key concept here is that your money is more like an orange than it is like math. It will erode and deteriorate over time, and no one is properly explaining to you how it will erode and why the use of math alone in a financial plan is an invalid approach to your financial needs, wants, and desires.

This is not to say that mathematics has no place in designing a financial strategy for your lifetime financial well-being. It does. It just cannot be the only function used to determine your wealth, happiness, and success. Other physical, economic, and human behavioral laws are needed to design a successful strategy for attaining, growing, and protecting your wealth at all times. The financial-planning industry today does not use or even consider using these necessary sciences to help design accurate programs.

LEAP takes into account all of these laws, and uses a more expert system of computation than simply using math alone. The financial professional who uses LEAP is trained to understand all of the properties of money and how money actually works in everyone's lifetime.

Eroding Factors

There are many ways in which money erodes, immediately when you receive it and over time. Therefore, you need intelligent defenses against these forces of destruction that act against your money. But before we look at how you can defend yourself, you must clearly understand what these forces are and how they work against you. The ten major factors that cause the value of your money to erode immediately and over time are:

1. inflation
2. taxes
3. technological change
4. planned obsolescence
5. financial expenses
6. lost-opportunity costs
7. interest-rate declines
8. stock-market declines
9. loans and interest charges
10. lawsuits

Let's look briefly at how each one of these factors will erode your wealth over time.

1. INFLATION

Inflation is the general increase in the price of goods and services that your money can be exchanged for or buy. Over time, the purchasing power of your money is eroded by inflation. An inflation rate of just 3 percent means that what costs $10,000 today will cost $10,300 next year or that your $10,000 next year will only be worth $9,700.

In thirty years, using only a 3 percent inflation rate, the same $10,000 would be worth only $4,120—a decline of 59 percent in purchasing power. This fact is a shock to most people who are trying to save for retirement. In later chapters of this book, you will see how your retirement savings plans are eroded, making it difficult for you to retire successfully without a defense against inflation.

People generally say that in order to keep up with inflation, your money should be earning at least the inflation rate annually—otherwise you are losing purchasing power. This is mathematically correct, but in reality it is wrong. For instance, inflation is not tax deductible. The government does not allow you to deduct its cost. So if your money is earning 3 percent taxable in a certificate of deposit (CD) and inflation is 3 percent, you are not keeping up. If there were no inflation, we would all be a lot richer.

2. TAXES

Taxes are one of the most serious wealth-eroding forces you face. The government uses tax revenue to operate. Tax laws are constantly changing, and no one knows what the future tax laws will be. Since the tax laws in the future are uncertain, any financial plan using today's tax laws to predict future outcomes is invalid and unreliable.

Before there was an income tax, many families were able to build up significant wealth. They were allowed to keep all that they earned.

When the federal income tax code was established in 1913, it was supposed to be temporary to help pay off accumulated government debt. As years have gone by, the public has discovered that the tax laws are not temporary and have become a permanent fixture on the economic and financial scene. When the tax laws started, the top marginal tax rate was only 7 percent. Now it is fluctuating between 30 percent and 40 percent.

The reasons for the continuation of income taxes have changed as well. The income tax has become a tool for the redistribution of wealth, through the creation of social programs, enhancement and enlargement of national defense, and much more.

A fundamental part of any financial plan is the need for a strategy to help prevent or minimize the effect of income taxes on your wealth. If you do not have such a plan, you will lose significant amounts of money that you may never be able to recapture. There are many income-tax-saving concepts you can use. Unfortunately, most people do not use any, and many use the wrong ones. A tax deferral is not a powerful weapon against income taxes; it only delays them. Many retirement savings plans today use this tax-deferred approach, and many people will be disappointed when they retire. I will cover this subject in depth later in this book.

There are many other taxes that you pay as well, such as state or province income taxes, city income taxes, sales taxes, excise taxes, Social Security taxes, and real estate taxes. They take another large portion of your earnings away from your wealth potential. When all of these taxes are taken into account, many people find themselves effectively in a 50 percent tax bracket—meaning that 50 percent of their annual earnings go to pay these various taxes—even those who earn low incomes. They just don't see all of the other taxes that are taking their money away. They only look at their paycheck and the income and other taxes that are withheld. If there were no taxes, we would all be very rich, no matter what level of income we earned.

I am always amazed that most people simply ignore the steps they can take to save taxes. As I said earlier, many people use the wrong approach of only deferring income taxes rather than minimizing or even eliminating these taxes through various means such as deductions, credits, or ways to recapture the taxes paid. I will discuss how to eliminate, reduce, or recapture income taxes throughout this book.

While taxes erode the value of your income and assets while you are alive, there is another tax that is looming at your death called the estate tax. Basically, over your lifetime, government takes an ongoing percentage of what you make and earn while you are alive, and then takes a percentage of what you have at your death. They get you both coming and going, literally.

Many financial and estate-planning advisors provide estate-tax advice. But from what I have seen, for the most part their planning is ineffective and can actually create greater losses of wealth for consumers than no planning at all. Estate planning is a critical component to building and protecting your wealth, and I'll discuss proper estate planning in chapter 8.

3. TECHNOLOGICAL CHANGES

The world is constantly changing. New technologies are replacing old ones, and many families spend a large portion of their annual income on updating their household technology, regardless of whether the physical asset itself has actually been exhausted. This leaves less money for saving, investing, and ultimately for wealth building.

For instance, the vast majority of families buy a new car only when their old car's useful life is over—the technology they acquire in the new car is secondary to them. But this is not so in the realm of consumer electronics. When DVDs supplanted videos as the main mode for viewing feature films at home on television, many families bought DVD players despite the fact that their videocassette players were in fine working order and that they could still buy or rent videos.

This technological consumption and turnover has a profound effect on anyone's ability to grow wealth. Since technological innovation is a predictable expense, one must account for its occurrence in any financial plan. It is an eroding factor of wealth and needs to be factored in when a person projects the need for money in the future.

Forty years ago, it was impossible for many people to even conceive of many of the consumer products that exist today. Cable television,

VCRs, DVDs, plasma and high-definition TVs, cell phones, personal computers, and automotive navigation systems are just some of the technological innovations that have occurred since the 1960s. Thousands of dollars are spent by the average family that simply never could have been predicted by a financial advisor developing a financial plan for a family in 1960 or 1970. Since the financial plans did not foresee these technological advancements and their costs, the public's retirement plans are failing today to keep up.

When designing a financial plan, expenditures for new technologies that are developed in the future must be included even though we do not know what they will be. Without addressing this planning element, as a retiree you will be expected not to participate in the next wave of technological innovation and the greatness of our future economy.

4. PLANNED OBSOLESCENCE

The "cousin" of technological change, planned obsolescence occurs when products are designed to have a shorter life span than what is possible. This results in a need to replace these products at regular intervals. Products are designed to have a life that is finite and known. Planned obsolescence allows manufacturers to have a follow-up market they can count on.

Every product you purchase has a life expectancy. Much of your current savings and investment is really only delayed expenditure. Not only does government have its eyes on your money, but corporations have their eyes on it too. They do a great job of getting consumers to repeatedly buy new products, sometimes even before the old products wear out. They can do this by changing style, color, or materials through persuasive advertising.

A plan that does not include consideration for future expenditures based on planned obsolescence and technological change is no plan at all. There must be a contingency for these most certain future expenditures. When you look at many financial plans in the financial services industry today, you will see no factoring for planned obsolescence. Such plans fall short of their intended targets.

5. FINANCIAL EXPENSES

What I mean by financial expenses are those costs charged for holding your money in a particular financial product or service. There are all kinds of financial expenses that you may incur when your money is accumulating in a particular insurance, savings, or investment vehicle. These financial expenses include fees, commissions, premiums, and charges. These costs are sometimes hidden and are usually not easy to calculate.

Fees are the most obvious. You may have an up-front fee, an inside fee, or a back-end fee. Whatever the reason for a fee to be charged, you need to understand that this fee is a wealth-eroding cost. Therefore, you need to evaluate whether the fee is worth paying before entering into the financial transaction. If you can get the same or better information or products without a fee, you would be better off. Fees are a serious cost to your wealth-building potential. Even if the advice were good, paying large fees for that advice can negate the long-term benefits of the plan.

I once saw a client who had hired a financial planner. The fee for the service was $5,000 to start and $1,000 for each annual review, going up by 3 percent each year for inflation. Over thirty years, if those fees had been invested, the client would have had hundreds of thousands of dollars extra. If the client had continued with that financial planner to age 85—and I know he hoped he would live that long—it would have cost him well over $1 million in lost investment opportunity.

So it is important to be efficient when selecting products and services and examining the financial expenses included in the transaction. The ones that you don't see may be just as wealth-eroding as the ones that you can see up front. All financial products or services have a cost or expense. These expenses have to be compared to the ultimate value you receive. The cheapest product or service may not be, and most often isn't, the best alternative. Sometimes the product with the highest commission or fee is the best alternative. A careful review of these financial costs and expenses is necessary since they will have a long-lasting effect on your wealth potential.

6. LOST-OPPORTUNITY COSTS

One of the least understood factors in wealth erosion—and probably the most rarely used by financial advisors—is the concept of lost-opportunity cost. Without considering this important wealth-eroding factor, it is almost impossible to produce an efficient financial plan. Lost-opportunity cost should be calculated in every financial transaction you make.

What is lost-opportunity cost? It is the actual money you lose as a result of making any particular financial decision as compared to another particular financial decision. In order to be considered a lost-opportunity cost, the money you lose must be an actual cost and not a hypothetical cost. Examples of a direct cost are financial fees, taxes, interest charges, or other payments for holding a financial product. Say you pay an income tax of $1,500 on an investment that you made. You do not only lose $1,500, you also lose the value of what that money would have been worth to you in the future. If you pay the same $1,500 every year for thirty years, the cost is not just $45,000, but $183,000, including the lost earnings on the money, assuming an 8 percent annual rate of return.

Another example of lost-opportunity costs on financial products is in the area of auto, homeowner's, or term life insurance policies. Now, I am not saying that you should not have these types of coverage because you may very well need them. But think of it this way: If you never had a claim on any of these policies, you would have a lost-opportunity cost on the premiums for all of the years of payments and beyond.

Say you have on average during your working career from age 21 to age 65 the following: an auto policy with a premium of $1,100, a homeowner's policy premium of $400, and a term life policy with a premium of $500. The total annual premiums are $2,000. If you never had a claim during those forty-five years, there would be a lost-opportunity cost that you incurred by not having that money working for you at 8 percent. The lost-opportunity cost would be $2,000 at 8 percent for forty-five years, for a total of $835,000. To age 85, it would grow to about $4,000,000. Keep in mind that these numbers do not reflect any increase in premiums due to inflation.

When you add up all of the expenses, costs, and taxes on all financial products in your lifetime, the lost-opportunity cost is in the multimillions of dollars. I have calculated that a typical family will incur between $5 million and $10 million in lost-opportunity cost in their lifetime. Therefore, it is important to identify these costs and learn how to minimize or avoid them in the future. **If people would spend more time trying to hold onto their money instead of spending so much time trying to find an investment to make money, they would be much better off.**

7. INTEREST-RATE DECLINES

The interest rate is the rate paid by one individual or entity to another individual or entity for the right to use money. When you deposit money into a bank, the bank is willing to pay you interest for the use of your money. In effect, you are lending the bank your money. If you anticipate receiving a certain interest rate on your investments to use as retirement income and the rate is substantially less when you actually retire, you may have difficulty making ends meet. This has happened to many people over the last decade. Interest-rate declines erode the value of your money by reducing the amount of money that it can earn. This is especially true if your wealth is locked into long-term investments at low interest rates during a time of high inflation and high taxes.

A retired person I know told me recently that if anyone had told him thirty years ago that he would have $1,000,000 when he retired, he would have thought that person was crazy. He could never have imagined having that much money. After all, statistics show that less than 1 percent of the population has that much in cash when they retire. But instead of being pleased with this outcome, he told me he was scared to death about his situation. He is only getting 3 percent on his saving account at the bank, so he has just $30,000 a year to live on in addition to his Social Security. He said that he could not imagine that $1,000,000 was not enough to live on over the course of his entire lifetime. He is afraid to invest money since he might lose it, and is worried about living too long and running out of money due to inflation.

This man was a victim of traditional thinking about money and financial planning. He was not aware that interest rates, tax rates, market rates, and inflation can all fluctuate to do damage on even what appears to be a substantial sum.

8. STOCK-MARKET DECLINES

Stock-market declines can have a huge eroding effect on your wealth. If you hold wealth in the stock market and your portfolio declines by 50 percent during a one-year period, it will take you more than seven years at 10 percent annual market growth just to get back to even. Given inflation and taxation, it could take even longer.

In this example, your original $10,000 investment would be worth $5,000 after a 50 percent decline. A 10 percent increase raises the value of your investment to $5,500; another 10 percent increases it to $6,050; after another year it would be up to $6,655; and so on. Remember, it takes a 100 percent increase to make up for a 50 percent decline.

But what if you are retired or have a child ready for college when the market drops and your money is gone? Again, many people experience such calamity in their lifetime and it is totally not necessary and can be avoided. You do not have to take risk in order to get high returns. Many advisors say, "Don't worry! It will come back in the long run." Keep in mind that no one should think about having their money work only in the long run. As the great economist John Maynard Keynes said, "We are all dead in the long run."

I will discuss how to minimize the impact of market declines and protect your money from these eroding factors in later chapters.

9. INTEREST CHARGES AND LOANS

It should be clear to everyone that if you are looking to make money in the form of interest earnings, then the reverse is true when you pay it out. The problem is that the rate of interest you pay out is almost always higher than the rate of interest you receive. For example, if someone has $5,000 in a bank, he may be earning 3 percent interest. That same person may have a car loan for $5,000 at the same bank and pay 6 percent interest. In effect, the consumer is borrowing his own money in this example and losing 3 percent for the totality of the transactions.

The next area of concern is credit-card borrowing. Credit cards have caused major financial crises in many families. Interest charges as high as 18 percent are devastating. If you could earn 18 percent on your money consistently, you would not need to read this book. So why pay it out? You need to know the best ways to borrow money when borrowing is necessary. This book will share with you many of the most efficient methods of borrowing, but keep in mind that, in general, borrowing of any kind is an eroding factor.

10. LAWSUITS

Finally, no matter how well you plan, unless you have full protection against creditors and lawsuits, your wealth could be eroded at any time. Accidents can happen to anyone. That is why they are called accidents. If you are at fault for creating an accident, even though you had no intention of causing any injury or damage to someone else, the laws are such that you will be liable to compensate financially any parties who have been injured or killed or whose property has been damaged. Lawsuits of up to $10 million for injury to another person are not uncommon. You may not be able to avoid accidents in your lifetime, but you can protect your wealth from being totally lost through sound planning techniques.

The key to this area is to have proper insurance coverage, hold assets in "safe harbors," and utilize those savings and investments that are exempt from creditors. I will discuss these items throughout the book.

A Sound Offense Is a Good Defense

Keep in mind that getting a high rate of return is not your only financial task. If you can beat the eroding factors, you will be very well on your way to financial success. **There is more money in the elimination of eroding factors than there is in finding the right investments.** The nice thing about this type of planning is that it is easier to get results, since the money already exists. It is your money that is being taken away from you. Protect it and watch over it. Remember, most people lose more than $5 million in their lifetime due to these various wealth-eroding factors. If you can learn how you are losing it and how to retrieve it, then your financial situation will be easier to manage.

> ## KEY POINTS
> • **Money is not math, and math is not money.**
> • **Eroding factors are the reason for most financial problems that people have—not investments.**
> • **The key to financial success is to avoid eroding factors, protect your money, and keep it working for you.**

CHAPTER 3
Inaccurate and Misleading Information

The world is rife with misinformation and bad advice. It seems that consumers are often much more willing to listen to someone with a compelling personality—as wrong as he or she may be—than to someone who truly knows the facts on how to build and manage personal wealth.

In your quest to build wealth, you will be bombarded with misinformation from newspapers, magazines, books, television, radio, and marketing and advertising materials. Many famous financial writers have been responsible for millions of dollars lost by consumers, while they continue to sell their CDs, videotapes, seminars, and/or their sponsors' products.

Even the best-intended information might be misguided if it is incomplete and only promotes the advantages of a particular financial product while ignoring its disadvantages. All too often, financial professionals suggest that consumers invest in a particular financial product without knowing or thinking about how that product will fit into the individual consumer's financial life. There is no financial product that can work alone to make anyone's financial life run smoothly. The key is to find the right combination of financial products and use them in a complementary fashion.

Let's now dig deeper and explore some reasons why you will receive financial misinformation or even bad advice from the media and in the financial services arena. It is important for you to know that the information you are reading or hearing is ill-advised and can damage your financial well-being.

From Misinformation to Bad Advice

When does misinformation turn into bad advice?

Misinformation turns into bad advice at the point when a consumer acts on the information provided without verification or evaluation as to its merits.

How can you know the difference between bad advice and sound advice?

Actually, it's quite easy if you have the right evaluation tools. But without the right gauges or measurement devices, which most people do not own, the job of recognizing and selecting sound advice becomes difficult. So where do you start to get the proper education? You must start with basic knowledge about decision making. There are two types of decision making: decision making based on deductive reasoning and decision making based on inductive reasoning.

Deductive reasoning may be simply defined as the ability to make a decision based on known facts that lead to a specific conclusion. For example, I have four oranges and I eat one. How many oranges do I have left? The answer is obvious: three. I had a set of known facts, and I deduced the answer from those facts. But what if I said, "I ate an orange. How many oranges do I have?" You could not know the answer because you do not know how many oranges there were in the first place. You could not deduce the answer unless you knew how many oranges there were to start.

On the other hand, the use of inductive reasoning does not require a complete set of facts before you can come to a conclusion or decision. In making decisions using inductive reasoning, you use facts you have and base your decision on the possibilities or alternative scenarios that can be derived from the known information. Such words as insight, perspective, sixth sense, logic, and common sense come to mind when discussing inductive reasoning. You can draw from a variety of skills or instincts to come to a conclusion and know what to do. You do not need a complete factual basis for your decision making, as you do when using deductive reasoning.

It is important to note that both deductive and inductive reasoning skills are necessary in our lives. Sometimes we need proof through a deductive process. Other times we can make a decision based on inductive reasoning without proof, because we somehow "know" the decision is correct.

When it comes to financial planning and structuring our financial lives, we need to use both types of reasoning. But most financial advisors today use only deductive reasoning, and that presents a major problem for consumers.

THE FALLACY OF USING ONLY DEDUCTIVE REASONING IN FINANCIAL PLANNING

The use of deductive reasoning by financial advisors is a major cause of misinformation that leads to bad advice. For instance, let's say you are interested in a retirement plan. A financial advisor using only deductive reasoning may ask you a series of questions, such as:

- **At what age do you want to retire?**
- **How much income will you need at retirement?**
- **How long do you think you will need that income?**
- **What is your risk tolerance?**

If these are the questions you are asked, you are dealing with an advisor who uses only deductive reasoning, and the plan he designs for you is not likely to work. He asked these questions in order to get a series of facts that are needed to use deductive reasoning to give you an easily quantifiable answer.

Without your responses to his questions, he would not be able to make the necessary mathematical calculations to prove to you what plan to buy. Without your responses, he would not know how to guide you or point you in the right direction. Only with your responses is he able to articulate a solution that goes something like this:

"If you need this much income at your retirement and all you have is this much money today, then you need to save and invest these dollars in our product today."

Remember what you learned already, that money is not math and math is not money. Anyone using deductive-reasoning analysis thinks that math and money are identical. They rely on math to provide you with answers and proof of the veracity of the plan. But no one can predict what will happen in the future—especially in the long term—or what the variables or mathematical assumptions should be. The plan designed from such logic is only good for one day. That's about it. Every day after the first day, the plan is going off course.

How do you know when you will retire? Does a 35-year-old person really know for sure that he will want to retire at age 65? He might change his mind and want to retire at age 55 because he feels burned out or bored at his job. His health may deteriorate and he may need to retire earlier because he is unable to work. On the other hand, he may decide at age 65 that work is still very meaningful and may wish to work until age 75 or even 85.

How do you know how much income you will need at retirement? What method did you use to determine that amount? Was it based on today's standards? Or did it just sound good?

Remember, you now know about the eroding factors of income taxes, lost-opportunity cost, planned obsolescence, technological change, inflation, market fluctuation, interest charges, and fluctuating interest rates. You may begin to see how difficult it really is to use deductive reasoning to determine a sound plan for retirement when these factors cannot be predicted with any accuracy. Most likely, whatever you think your income needs will be at retirement, they are likely to be much higher. Would you really want to limit yourself to a specified income based on today's assumptions, knowing that tomorrow's income needs will be a lot different?

How are you supposed to answer the following question: "How long will you need the income during your retirement years?" Do you just take a life expectancy chart and guess? What if you live to 105—will the plan work or do you simply fold up your tent and starve because you ran out of money? What about your children—do they spend their money to take care of you?

EVER-CHANGING VARIABLES

Will the mathematical variables used to create deductive-reasoning-type financial plans stay constant in order for you to reach your goal, meet your need, or hit your target? Of course not! So why pretend from the beginning that the assumptions used in the plan have any merit at all? When you see or read financial-planning advice that uses interest rates, investment rates, income-tax rates, inflation rates, along with a timetable for the plan, you now know that these assumptions are certain to change and so, too, will the outcome of the plan.

The big question to answer is, if these variables are going to change, then why should anyone consider it to be a viable plan in the first place? Each year, the plan will become more outmoded and the end result will be far off the mark. The excuse I hear most from advisors who use this type of deductive-reasoning planning is that they will review and update the plan and recalculate, using the then-current assumptions. In effect, they are admitting that the first plan was off target, and that each and every other yearly plan will be off target. They have to keep readjusting the plan to keep it supposedly on course. The problem is that the plan will not be able to be readjusted because of the time that is being lost each year. It is much more difficult to adjust a plan in the short run than in the long run and have it succeed.

For example, say that you are now age 60 and the plan is on course. What happens if in the next year interest rates drop far below the assumptions used for retirement income, or the stock market declines, or income-tax rates double, or you get sued, or inflation is roaring away at double digits? You only have four years left to update and review the plan, and it will be almost impossible for you to be able to readjust the plan to meet your needs in only a short window of opportunity.

Can you imagine NASA shooting a rocket to the moon knowing that the path is wrong and having to keep readjusting the path to get the rocket to the target? NASA would never plan a mission the way financial advisors plan for the public. NASA maps out a successful course and then has many backup systems and built-in redundancies to better assure success of the mission. Financial planners do not use backup systems or built-in redundancies to make sure that you will overcome the constantly changing eroding factors.

Deductive-reasoning-type plans and the update-and-review strategy won't work. You are either going to run out of time or run out of money. Since time is one of the variables used in building any plan, the plan becomes harder and harder to achieve as people get older and a variable like a market decline occurs between reviews. Many people now in their 50s or 60s have retirement savings plans that have been decimated by the market decline of 2000 to 2003. Because of the short time left until their planned retirement, their plans can't be fixed, and today they are in financial trouble.

Money, Fortune, and *Forbes* magazines all ran articles in 2002 and 2003 on how people were unable to retire even though they had a financial plan designed by a licensed financial planner. Instead of blaming the financial-planning theory, it was the stock market that got the blame. Some financial planners state: "Who could have imagined that the stock market would go down that much [from 2000 to 2002] all at once?"

The public took their medicine and went along with this feeble excuse. Yet all along it was the financial-planning theory that caused their misery and not the stock market. Sound planning theory would not let that happen. The financial planners quoted in these articles suggested that these folks should either lower their standard of living, reduce their income targets for retirement, move to a cheaper city, town, state, or province, work five years longer than desired, or invest more money into the stock market so when it comes back they will be able to retire. The people who followed that advice are still waiting.

In summary, deductive-reasoning-type planning has much inefficiency and has little chance of helping people succeed in meeting their full financial potential and financial success.

THE IMPORTANCE OF INDUCTIVE REASONING IN YOUR FINANCIAL PLAN

Inductive-reasoning-based planning works on the assumption that no one can predict the future or can control the interest rates, tax rates, market rates, loan rates, inflation rates, etc. All that is certain about the future is that it will be very different from today. These are inductive thoughts. All of the economic variables in the future will be changing and out of your control. The stock market might go down for several years in a row just as you are about to retire. Income-tax rates may go up substantially as the baby boomer generation retires. Your retirement savings plan may not be available to you when you want to retire because the government might change the minimum age of distribution, as some legislators are now suggesting. Will your plan hold up under any set of circumstances?

As when NASA sends a man to the moon, all contingencies must be planned for and every variable expected to change. The plan must have built-in redundancies and a fail-safe system. These thoughts will help you prepare for your financial future.

Remember, you do not wear a seat belt in your car every day because you think you are going to crash. You wear it in case you do. The same thinking must be incorporated into all of your money decisions. You hope nothing ever happens, but if it does, you need a plan that will work under that scenario.

Inductive planning looks into the future with "new eyes" and with optimism. Deductive planning uses past performance of products, average rates of return, average past inflation rates, and average market conditions. The future is not a mirror of the past, but rather a magic carpet ride of hope and aspirations. Your financial plan should not be based on past performance and limitations as to your anticipated needs. You should have your money reaching for maximum performance, maximum efficiency, and maximum effective results that protect against the many eroding factors and all of the unknowns.

Inductive planning does not limit your financial potential to only meeting your anticipated needs. It allows for an increased standard of living so that wants and desires can be achieved as well.

There are two possible roads you can take. One road limits you to a set of predesigned needs, goals, or targets and hopes that the variables don't change too much over time. The other road is to build a plan that seeks to maximize the performance of your income and your assets and to maximize your opportunity to surpass your needs, goals, and targets while protecting you from the eroding factors. The choice is obvious. Most people would take the second choice. They just don't know that such a choice is available to them.

Good Advice

How can you recognize good advice and sound information? First, understand that every financial product has advantages and disadvantages. No one product can do it all, and no one product has all positive features.

If the information you receive about a product just touts the product's advantages, and there is not a complete and thorough explanation of the disadvantages, you know that you are being given incomplete information and possibly bad advice. Anyone can make something sound good by telling only one side of the story, but it takes two sides of the story to fully understand the product or service you are considering for your financial life.

Remember, it is the enhancement of a financial product's advantages and the elimination or reduction of the disadvantages that ultimately make for a sound and successful financial strategy. What good is it to have a financial plan that doesn't compensate for the disadvantages of the financial products used to fulfill the plan's goals?

The key to financial success is not to have money in one financial product for college education, other money in one financial product for retirement, other money in one financial product for wealth building, and other money for estate planning. This financial-planning concept of having each dollar work separately is one of the core reasons for financial failure for many people.

Money needs to work in concert. You need to develop a holistic view of your financial life, with all of your assets working like a symphony orchestra rather than a one-man band. Your assets and money should all be coordinated and integrated to formulate one offensive and defensive plan. Money should be flowing from one financial product to another in a strategic manner that yields high rates of return, low risk, and more protection. Keeping money isolated in financial products to compound or grow is inefficient and ineffective. Singular financial-product planning for each need, goal, or target can result in a loss of your overall wealth potential.

KEY POINTS

- There is much financial misinformation provided in the media and financial services arena.
- Financial assumptions used in financial planning cannot be controlled or predicted.
- A sound financial plan takes into consideration both deductive and inductive reasoning.
- Every financial product has advantages and disadvantages. You need to know both.

CHAPTER 4

Winning Strategy

If sound financial planning were merely a matter of discipline to save and invest money over the long run, everyone's financial plan would work successfully. Unfortunately, it simply is not that easy, and the current state of financial planning does not contain all of the components that lead to a successful plan. Let's review the reasons why so many people fail financially even if they plan.

- **First,** some people are not able to save or invest enough money to reach the plan's required targets.
- **Second,** many people do not have the ability to continually receive the rate of return on their savings and investments in the plan's design.
- **Third,** some people will lose money in the stock market or other investments.
- **Fourth,** people end up needing to spend some of their money before it has time to fully accumulate toward their financial goals.
- **Fifth,** many people are searching for a single financial product that will do the job, instead of building a coordinated process that uses many financial products coordinated and integrated together.
- **Sixth,** and most important, the eroding factors of taxes, inflation, planned obsolescence, technological change, market fluctuations, interest-rate fluctuations, interest charges, lawsuits, etc., may all take their toll and work hard to reduce wealth accumulation.

It should make sense that if there were only one financial product that could make everyone's financial plan successful, everyone would own it by now. For more than 100 years, people have made the same mistake over and over again, looking for the magic financial product that will make them either rich or financially successful. There would not be so many choices of mutual funds if there were one mutual fund that could be depended on to work all the time. There would not be a need for modern portfolio theory or asset allocation if there were one portfolio that was sure to provide reliable returns. But even if there were one product or one portfolio that was right for everyone, just putting money away and accumulating it in that product for one's future financial needs, goals, and desires would still not work effectively.

The process of building wealth needs both an offense and a defense. Between the two, it is the defense that is much more important than the offense. And that basically is the problem: Too many people concentrate their financial life on the offense (accumulation) and ignore the defense (protection).

What can you do to avoid the same mistakes that most people make and find a successful financial result? You need to know how to use your money and not just where to put it. By the "how," I mean saving and investing your money in the most productive, efficient, and effective manner. Over a lifetime, understanding and avoiding all of the financial pitfalls and overcoming the eroding factors is the most powerful financial strategy you can utilize to successfully build and protect your wealth.

"Where" you put your money will become less and less important than "how" your money works in the process; that is the real winning factor.

You must always remember the big lesson in chapter 1 of this book. There are three influences in your financial world: (1) financial institutions, (2) government, and (3) corporations.

Financial institutions follow the four rules of wanting your money, wanting it on a systematic basis, holding your money for as long as possible, and convincing you not to take it all out at once. The government has the power to get your money by taxing it and regulating its use. Corporations build and make products that you need and want, but also plan to get more of your money by having those products break down or by making new and improved ones.

What powers do you have over your money once you begin to save and invest it? Very little if you let financial institutions, government, and corporations become your financial partners! You need to tap into your own power over your own income and assets. You have a great power, but most people relinquish their power unknowingly. They put their money into financial products, give up the control, and hope for a successful result. Like any casino, the odds are against you, and only a few will win. **You must control your money at all times, learning to use it over and over again, getting more than one use out of each dollar. That is the only winning strategy.**

Strategy, Not Product

Notice that I use the term "strategy" as opposed to "product," "goal," or "objective." Many financial advisors use the words "need," "goal," or "objective" in order to design your financial plan. What good is setting financial needs, goals, and objectives if the wrong use of money or strategy is used for the journey? Most of the financial literature, advertising, and marketing make appeals for you to first establish your financial needs, goals, or objectives. This methodology is wrong. In so doing, they are asking you to concentrate your efforts on the ends rather than the means. **By focusing on the ends—needs, goals, or objectives—one can lose sight of the means—or the best methods—for reaching your financial potential.**

Sure, we all know that we need money in the future for such things as a new home, college tuition for our children, retirement, or an estate plan. But what is the best way to get to these goals? Trying to predict the exact amount of money needed may sound easy, but it is almost impossible to do. Why do so many people pretend it can be done? And why put limits on your financial future anyway when it is impossible to predict?

Let's look at why using the ends, rather than the means, as a primary design tool for a financial plan is incomplete. All we have to do is study and understand our own capitalist society and contrast it with the economics of a communist society. Karl Marx said it all in *The Communist Manifesto*, the bible of communism, when he said, "Each according to his need, each according to his ability." In other words, no individual in a society should have more than what he or she needs, and each person should contribute to the good of all based on his or her ability to work and earn money.

That type of society has failed over and over again in history because it is based on first establishing people's needs and then building a planned society to meet those needs. It does not consider the fact that needs and the world change over time. It fails also because the means to get to the goal of meeting everyone's needs are always inefficient and ineffective, so the goals are never reached. Communism is the ultimate example of using only deductive reasoning to create an economic plan.

There is a parallel between a communist society's tendency to create an economic plan and the tendency of many financial advisors to use only deductive reasoning when designing financial plans for clients. This leads in many ways to the same end result—failure to reach a society's or an individual's full financial potential. **And deductive financial planning fails individuals for many of the same reasons communism has failed entire societies: the inability to take into account changes that occur in the world over time, changes in personal needs over time, and the inefficient and ineffective use of resources.**

On the other hand, Adam Smith, the father of capitalism and author of *The Wealth of Nations*, wrote about the "invisible hand" of the market. He said that there should not be a financial plan, but trust that the drive toward profits will lead each one of us to use our money (limited resources) in the most efficient and effective manner. Capitalism has proven that an unplanned society succeeds where the planned societies of communism fail. **You too should focus on controlling the efficient and effective use of your limited supply of money rather than relinquishing its use to a targeted need or goal.**

Four Rules for Personal Financial Success

Just as financial service institutions have four rules they try to follow in order to maximize their financial well-being, you can take advantage of four rules in order to be a successful capitalist. These rules will allow you to create a winning strategy to defend against and counteract the factors that erode money in order to build and protect your wealth.

1. **Money is a commodity; it is not simply a number.**
2. **Money is precious and finite; it must be treated as a precious commodity and protected against all eroding factors.**
3. **Money must be used efficiently and effectively; it must not be left to just accumulate over time, nor should it be set aside for just one purpose.**

4. Money must be respected and must be put to work for the good of society as well as for your own financial future.

Only when you understand that money is a scarce resource and a commodity can you fully understand why you need to develop a better strategy for lifelong financial success. If you think it is only mathematical, you will most likely not reach your full financial potential.

MAKE SURE MONEY SERVES MULTIPLE PURPOSES

The key to successfully building and protecting your wealth is to have your money do more than one job. You should strive to make each dollar serve two, three, or even four purposes. Although none of us has the financial power of a bank or other financial institution, you can use the same principles to make your money work more productively, efficiently, and effectively. The reality is that even if money is earning a decent rate of return, it may not be working for you as powerfully as it should be.

Only when money stays in motion, being put to several different uses and flowing through your personal financial model like blood through your body, will you have successful results. By using the motion of money, you can use your limited resources to perform multiple tasks and produce multiple benefits. This principle is called the "Motion of Money in Personal Finance" and is the major strategy used in the Lifetime Economic Acceleration Process (LEAP).

The Winning Strategy: The Motion of Money

The winning strategy of the motion of money in personal finance cannot be attained or found in any single financial product. Rather, this winning strategy is one that coordinates and integrates the use of multiple financial products and has the money flowing freely among them. Since every financial product has advantages and disadvantages, this strategy helps accentuate the advantages while minimizing or even eliminating the disadvantages.

An analogy I like to use to help explain the concept of the coordination and integration of financial products' advantages and the elimination of their disadvantages can be found in the world of nature. Oxygen is a gas, and too much oxygen in your body will kill you. Hydrogen is also a gas, and too much hydrogen in your body will kill you. But when they are combined in the proper proportion, oxygen and hydrogen make up water, which is the basis for all life on our planet.

In a similar way, a single financial product in too large a concentration can leave you in a dangerous financial position and severely damage your ability to attain, grow, and protect your wealth. But two or more separate products coming together at the right time and in the right mix can help you attain substantial success in your quest for a lifetime of wealth building.

In the following chapters I will discuss in depth the advantages and disadvantages of numerous financial products and services, and I'll take you through examples of coordination strategies that enhance the advantages of financial products while minimizing or eliminating the disadvantages.

KEY POINTS

- It is not where you put your money that counts; it is more important to know how to use it.
- Each dollar must be used to provide multiple purposes. Avoid one use of your dollars.
- No product can work effectively alone. Financial products must be coordinated and integrated with each other.

CHAPTER 5

Compounding

You have often heard that you should let your money compound over time. It is perhaps the single most well-known piece of "conventional wisdom" in the personal finance pantheon. Pick up any financial magazine, newspaper, advertisement, or brochure and you will read about how compounding can work for you. Unfortunately, compounding is not all it is cracked up to be.

Sure, there are some advantages to compounding, especially in the short run, but the longer you compound, the more likely it is that serious financial problems will occur. This chapter will provide you with the information you need in order to take control of your wealth-building potential by utilizing compounding more wisely.

The main advantage of compounding is that your money earns more money for you the longer you compound it. Interest begets interest and grows in an exponential manner. But I am not writing this book to tell you what you already know. You need all information, not just the advantages. Compounding has many disadvantages, and it is important for you to understand them in order to mitigate their negative effects on your wealth-building goals.

The most devastating use of compounding is in taxable or tax-deferred accounts such as savings accounts, money-market accounts, deferred annuities, mutual funds, or pretax retirement savings plans. It is essential to understand why compounding your money in these types of accounts can actually lower your overall rate of return.

You may be thinking, "How could compounding one's money be bad when almost everyone is using it and promoting its use?" It is because you are only being shown the advantages, while the disadvantages and dangers are being hidden or ignored. The proponents of compounding often show a pictorial or visual called a "mountain chart." The mountain chart shows graphically how one's money may look as it compounds year after year. It shows columns of numbers showing the amount of money getting larger and larger because of the compounding effect. This is a very powerful marketing tool, since it gives people a sense that they will make more money over time through compounding. But let's look at compounding a little more carefully.

Figure 5.1 is a mountain chart that shows an investment of $10,000 with an 8 percent annual compounded rate of return. Notice that the account grows slowly from years 1 through 10, picks up speed from years 11 through 20, and really takes off in years 21 through 30. These three phases of compounding are called the accumulation, growth, and takeoff phases. Notice that a large portion of the growth takes place during the later stage, in the takeoff phase. It is these last five years that are responsible for a large portion of the growth of the money. The path of the mountain chart depicts what is called an "exponential curve," an upward slope that increases its angle like a ski jump. What conclusions can be drawn from the exponential curve?

- **First,** compounding your money does not work in a straight line.
- **Second,** most of the growth happens at the later stages of compounding.
- **Third,** no withdrawals can be made from the account if it is to achieve the results shown.
- **Fourth,** if any year is missed in the compounding process, one will lose money from the back end of the slope. It is like going down a big slide.
- **Fifth,** if a person tries to start saving money for retirement at age 55 and retires at age 65, that person will experience only the accumulation phase of the process and not reach either the growth or takeoff phases.

Figure 5.1: $10,000 Compounded at 8% a Year for 30 Years

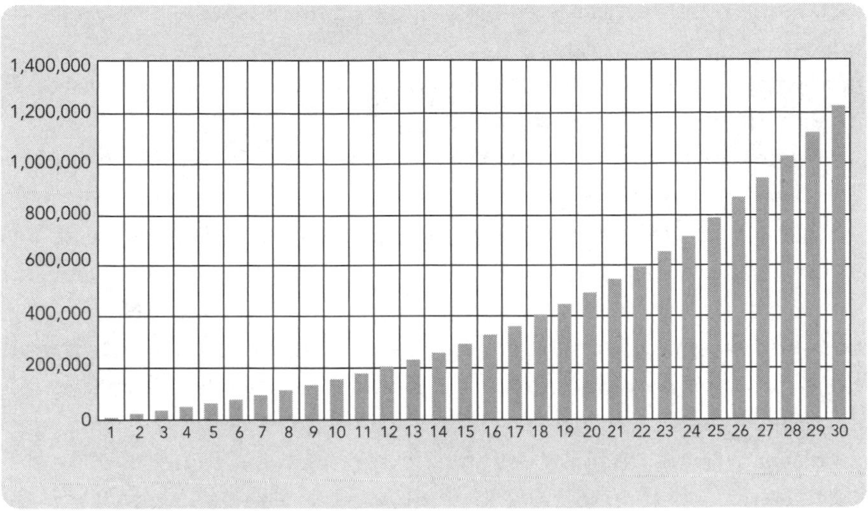

One Lifetime Exponential Curve

We are all born with only one exponential curve. We have a thirty- to forty-year curve the day we start to work. Most people waste their own power to build wealth by never utilizing their exponential curve potential. They start saving too late, leaving themselves either in the accumulation phase or the growth phase. Or they pull out money and slide down the slide. But even if your money reaches the takeoff phase of the exponential curve, you may still not be making any money, or getting your money to reach its full financial potential. **Although the mountain chart is very impressive and makes you believe you have made money, it does not reveal the true costs and expenses that can erode your wealth over time.**

Let me start with an analogy as an explanation. If a businessman has annual sales of $1 million, can we say that his business made money or was profitable? No, we would need to know his business costs as well as his income. If his costs were $1 million too, we would say his business broke even but was not profitable. If his costs were $1.2 million, we would have to say he operated at a loss. So the information on how much money the business made is not relevant until we know how much money he spent to get to that point.

The same holds true for any financial strategy you employ, including compound interest. We need to know not only how much money you will have at a point in time, but we need to know the financial costs you incurred in order to get there. It is precisely these costs that are not properly revealed to consumers. As a matter of fact, in almost every case they are hidden. As you will see, these costs are substantial, and over time may erode much if not all of your money.

Figure 5.2 illustrates what a $10,000 taxable savings account would be worth each year for thirty years at interest rates of 2, 4, 6, 8, and 10 percent.

As you can see, and mathematically speaking, it is a fact that the longer you compound, the more your money will earn. But we must keep in mind that "money is not math and math is not money." **Money is a commodity and it has eroding properties. Math is an abstract and does not have eroding properties. And therein lies the problem.**

Advocates of compounding your money use the "theory of compound numbers" in order to make you think that money will compound like the numbers will compound in math. They want you to believe that money is like math and math is like money. They are not sharing with you any information about the manner in which your money will be eroded over time.

The balance of this chapter will show you the effect of these eroding factors on any money that is compounding over time. Then when you understand both the advantages and disadvantages of compounding, you will be able to make more informed choices about where to put your money and how to use it properly.

The Effect of Taxes on Compound Accounts

Let's take a look at an example of how income taxes affect your attempts to build wealth through compounding your money.

Figure 5.3 (page 42) shows a $10,000 savings account, compounded at 6 percent annually for thirty years, and assumes the account holder is in the 30 percent marginal federal income tax bracket. Column 1 shows the gross value of the account in each year, column 2 shows the interest earned each year, and column 3 shows the amount of tax paid each year.

You can see that the gross value of the account grew to $57,435. Now look at the total taxes paid in column 3. It is $14,230. Now ask: "How were those taxes paid if the account compounded and had no withdrawals from it?"

The taxes were not paid from the account, since that would have lowered the account value all along. The answer is that they were paid out of earned income or by liquidating some other asset.

Figure 5.2: $10,000 Compounded at Various Interest Rates

YEAR	2%	4%	6%	8%	10%
1	10,200	10,400	10,600	10,800	11,000
2	10,404	10,816	11,236	11,664	12,100
3	10,612	11,249	11,910	12,597	13,310
4	10,824	11,699	12,625	13,605	14,641
5	11,041	12,167	13,382	14,693	16,105
6	11,262	12,653	14,185	15,869	17,716
7	11,487	13,159	15,036	17,138	19,487
8	11,717	13,686	15,938	18,509	21,436
9	11,951	14,233	16,895	19,990	23,579
10	12,190	14,802	17,908	21,589	25,937
11	12,434	15,395	18,983	23,316	28,531
12	12,682	16,010	20,122	25,182	31,384
13	12,936	16,651	21,329	27,196	34,523
14	13,195	17,317	22,609	29,372	37,975
15	13,459	18,009	23,966	31,722	41,772
16	13,728	18,730	25,404	34,259	45,950
17	14,002	19,479	26,928	37,000	50,545
18	14,282	20,258	28,543	39,960	55,599
19	14,568	21,068	30,256	43,157	61,159
20	14,859	21,911	32,071	46,610	67,275
21	15,157	22,788	33,996	50,338	74,002
22	15,460	23,699	36,035	54,365	81,403
23	15,769	24,647	38,197	58,715	89,543
24	16,084	25,633	40,489	63,412	98,497
25	16,406	26,658	42,919	68,485	108,347
26	16,734	27,725	45,494	73,964	119,182
27	17,069	28,834	48,223	79,881	131,100
28	17,410	29,987	51,117	86,271	144,210
29	17,758	31,187	54,184	93,173	158,631
30	18,114	32,434	57,435	100,627	174,494
TOTAL	18,114	32,434	57,435	100,627	174,494

Let's take a look at another chart, **Figure 5.4** (page 43), called "netting," where the taxes are paid from the account itself.

When the account is compounded, the total tax paid to the government is $14,230. When the account is netted, the total tax paid is only $10,439. Why is that?

The answer is that the netted account is being reduced each year by withdrawing the tax to be paid each year. That lowers the earnings each year and therefore lowers the tax. When you use compounding, you will always pay more in taxes.

By now you might be saying, "Okay, I understand the tax consequences

Figure 5.3: $10,000 Compounded at 6%, Out-of-Pocket Tax Cost

YEAR	END OF YEAR	1099 FORM	OUT-OF-POCKET TAX COST
1	10,600	600.00	(180.00)
2	11,236	636.00	(190.80)
3	11,910	674.16	(202.25)
4	12,625	714.61	(214,38)
5	13,382	757.49	(227.25)
6	14,185	802.94	(240.88)
7	15,036	851.11	(255.33)
8	15,938	902.18	(270.65)
9	16,895	956.31	(286.89)
10	17,908	1,013.69	(304.11)
11	18,983	1,074.51	(322.35)
12	20,122	1,138.98	(341.69)
13	21,329	1,207.32	(362.20)
14	22,609	1,279.76	(383.93)
15	23,966	1,356.54	(406.96)
16	25,404	1,437.93	(431.38)
17	26,928	1,524.21	(457.26)
18	28,543	1,615.66	(484.70)
19	30,256	1,712.60	(513.78)
20	32,071	1,815.36	(544.61)
21	33,996	1,924.28	(577.28)
22	36,035	2,039.74	(611.92)
23	38,197	2,162.12	(648.64)
24	40,489	2,291.85	(687.55)
25	42,919	2,429.36	(728.81)
26	45,494	2,575.12	(772.54)
27	48,223	2,729.63	(818.89)
28	51,117	2,893.41	(868.02)
29	54,184	3,067.01	(920.10)
30	57,435	3,251.01	(975.31)
TOTAL	57,435	47,435	(14,230)

of compounding in taxable savings or investments, but what if I am compounding my interest in a retirement savings plan or an annuity?" You might say that you don't pay taxes on those accounts while compounding and you might be in a lower tax bracket later when you withdraw the money.

The truth is that you will pay a larger amount of taxes when you defer them than if you paid them as you went along. The reason is that the tax liability from being deferred is also compounding. It is like building up a big IOU to the government. Remember that these plans are tax-deferral plans, not tax-elimination plans.

Figure 5.4: $10,000 Compounded at 6%, Net of Taxes

YEAR	@ 4.20% NEW INTEREST	CUMULATIVE TAXES
1	10,420	180
2	10,858	368
3	11,314	563
4	11,780	767
5	12,284	979
6	12,800	1,200
7	13,337	1,430
8	13,898	1,670
9	14,481	1,921
10	15,080	2,181
11	15,723	2,453
12	16,884	2,736
13	17,072	3,031
14	17,789	3,338
15	18,536	3,658
16	19,315	3,992
17	20,126	4,340
18	20,971	4,702
19	21,852	5,079
20	22,770	5,473
21	23,726	5,883
22	24,722	6,310
23	25,761	6,755
24	26,843	7,218
25	27,970	7,701
26	29,145	8,205
27	30,369	8,730
28	31,644	9,276
29	32,973	9,846
30	34,358	10,439
TOTAL	34,358	10,439

There is no doubt that netting a taxable account is better than compounding a taxable account, and that compounding money in a tax-deferred retirement plan is better than compounding outside of a retirement plan. The reality is that neither netting an account, compounding an account, nor tax-deferred accounts are among the most productive and efficient ways to grow your money. They all have many disadvantages that need to be understood in order to design the proper planning of your life savings and investments. We will discuss that in a later chapter.

A compounding account would be a better scenario if there are no taxes due on the interest or growth in the future. There are a few invest-ment vehicles that offer tax-free compounding. These include Roth IRAs in the United States, as well as permanent life insurance policies and tax-free municipal bonds.

The Effect of Inflation on Compounded Accounts

Inflation is similar to a tax. The only difference is that income taxes erode your money directly, while inflation erodes your money indirectly. Let's examine how inflation adversely affects your ability to build wealth through compounding.

Say inflation is running at an average annual rate of 3 percent. If the cost to run your household this year is $50,000, next year it will cost you $51,500. The year after that it will cost you $53,045. And the year after that it will cost you $54,636, and so on.

So let's see how this affects a $10,000 account invested at 6 percent that is compounding.

Figure 5.5 shows the impact of inflation on a $10,000 account com-pounding at 6 percent over 30 years.

As you can see, the effect of 3 percent annual inflation over 30 years is quite staggering. Whenever you see a mountain chart that shows values in the future, it is all irrelevant unless it is accompanied by the effect of the eroding factor of inflation. It does not matter how much mathematical value the chart shows you will have; it only matters what the money will buy in the future. **The use of compounding infor-mation that does not show the effects inflation will have on the account is one of the main reasons why most people fail to have a successful retirement plan, because inflation has not been properly taken into account.**

A word of caution is warranted when reviewing inflation rates and projecting these rates for planning purposes. The current consumer price index (CPI) is not necessarily a reliable source to use for planning pur-poses. The truth is that every individual or family has a different inflation rate, because inflation concerns the specific things you buy. The inflation rate will also fluctuate from year to year.

A person who works from home has a different inflation rate than a person who commutes 80 miles round-trip by car. A renter has a differ-ent inflation rate than a homeowner. A homeowner in one town has a dif-ferent inflation rate than a homeowner in another town, depending on

Figure 5.5: $10,000 Compounded at 6%, After 3% Annual Inflation

YEAR	ACCT. BALANCE END OF YEAR	TRUE VALUE
1	10,600	10,291
2	11,236	10,591
3	11,910	10,899
4	12,625	11,217
5	13,382	11,544
6	14,185	11,880
7	15,036	12,226
8	15,938	12,582
9	16,895	12,948
10	17,908	13,326
11	18,983	13,714
12	20,122	14,113
13	21,329	14,524
14	22,609	14,947
15	23,966	15,383
16	25,404	15,831
17	26,928	16,292
18	28,543	16,766
19	30,256	17,255
20	32,071	17,757
21	33,996	18,274
22	36,035	18,807
23	38,197	19,354
24	40,489	19,918
25	42,919	20,498
26	45,494	21,095
27	48,223	21,710
28	51,117	22,342
29	54,184	22,993
30	57,435	23,662

property taxes in the two communities. A person with a chronic illness that requires seven different medications daily has a different inflation rate than a person who only uses one prescription medication. We know for sure that there will be inflation in the future and that it will erode your money's purchasing power whenever it is withdrawn.

Lost-Opportunity Cost of Taxes Paid on Compounded Accounts

Do you remember the definition of lost-opportunity cost from chapter 2? Lost-opportunity cost is the loss of future value you incur as the result of a direct financial cost, such as taxes, interest, or other payments for owning or holding a financial product. When you pay an income tax on the compounding account, that tax payment is a direct expense of carrying that compounded account. Most people understand that a tax is a cost. But what many people fail to realize is that a tax payment also creates another cost. That cost is called the lost-opportunity cost on tax (LOC).

In order to understand this LOC, glance back for a moment to **Figure 5.3.** The total tax paid over thirty years is $14,230. That money paid in taxes also lost its opportunity to earn money for the account holder. His costs can be summarized as the original cost of $10,000, a series of tax payments over thirty years amounting to $14,230, and the lost opportunity cost of not having those tax dollars to invest forever. If the account had been tax-free at 6 percent, the account would have been worth the same $54,184. But the account holder would not have had to give the government any taxes. The account holder could have invested those dollars back into the same tax-free account, making the account worth $85,199. Therefore, the tax and LOC is $31,015.

The account holder could use that money for all sorts of things if he didn't have to make tax payments. He might want to use that money to pay off short-term loans at 10 percent. He might want to invest that money in life insurance or real estate.

The Long and the Short of Compounding

So, is compounding good or is it bad?

The answer, as with any financial instrument, is that compounding is useful for some people and not for others. But compounding should not be a goal unto itself. You should not fall into the trap of believing that compounding is a "miracle" for all people regardless of their situation.

I would agree that compounding should be used for money that you know has a specific, designated use in the relatively short term (no more than three to five years). For instance, say you have teenage children and want to get money out of investments that may fluctuate greatly when you need the money for college tuition. There is nothing wrong with putting that money in timed interest-bearing savings and compounding the interest for just a few years.

So let's get into the main problems of compounding:

1. Your money is only performing one job and getting one use.
2. Your money is acting inefficiently by not getting multiple benefits.
3. You are paying compound taxes on the earnings, either now or later.
4. There is a large lost-opportunity cost on taxes paid now.
5. You have no health benefits, disability benefits, death benefits, or creditor-suit protection from the compounding taxable account.

The positive side of compounding can be easily explained. Compounding your money can make it grow, keep it safe from loss, provide liquidity, and help meet short-term financial needs. However, you must be made aware of the negatives and how they work against you in order to negate their effects.

In summary, when compounding, your money is only working once and only receiving the gross interest rate of the account. Working against it is the impact of all the eroding factors such as income taxes, inflation, and lost-opportunity costs. The latter may very well wipe out a substantial portion of the total value of the account's growth over time.

Only through a complete understanding of the principle of compounding will you be able to determine whether compounding is an appropriate or inappropriate strategy for your own individual financial situation.

KEY POINTS

- Compounding interest creates compound tax.
- Compounding money only gives you one use of your money.
- Compounding in taxable savings or investments causes a lost-opportunity cost on the taxes paid.
- Compounding is best used in the short run.

CHAPTER 6

Taxable Investments

Investing money is quite different from saving money. Saving money has to do with the accumulation of money, whereby the principal is either insured or guaranteed, earns interest, and is readily available for use. Investing money, on the other hand, is the exact opposite.

When you invest money, you are looking for it to grow, not just to accumulate. The biggest difference between saving and investing is the risk factor. The principal in a savings vehicle is either stable, guaranteed, and/or insured. In an investment, the principal is rarely insured or guaranteed and will fluctuate up and down. There is a possibility that you will lose money.

The reason you accept this risk is that you believe there is the possibility that the rate of return on your money will be greater than it would be in a guaranteed, insured savings vehicle; otherwise, there would be few reasons to invest.

Risk cannot be eliminated from investing because it is the very nature of investing. People sometimes minimize or overlook the aspect of risk because they may be overly optimistic about their investment. But as Murphy's Law states, "What can go wrong probably will go wrong." Keep in mind that Murphy was a smart fellow.

There are a number of financial strategies you can employ to reduce risk on any given investment or portfolio of investments you may own. This is extremely important and seldom understood by consumers or even their financial advisors, because no one wants to be defensive or pessimistic about their investments at the start. They have a tendency to think that their investments will go up in value and that it is bad luck to assume they might go down. However, in investing as in sports, a good offense is having a good defense.

Amounts of Risk

Any investment can be categorized by the amount of risk involved in that investment. Investments may be categorized as having small, medium, or large risk; or having low, medium, or high risk. Notice that there is not a category that has "no risk." Yet that is how many people enter into the realm of investing: as if there were no risk.

One of the unfortunate theories you will hear in the investment world is "the higher or larger the risk, the greater the reward." Conversely, "the smaller the risk involved, the lower the reward." Since most people want a high rate of return, they often are lured into making investments with high risk attached to them. Often, people will find an investment that had a high rate of return in the past, one that outperformed all or many others, and invest in it with the anticipation that it will continue to grow at the same rate, only to discover that it becomes the worst-performing investment after they buy it.

Past performance is no indication of future performance, and investors are warned of this fact over and over again. But past performance is still being used today as one of the measures to evaluate new investments.

Some financial advisors use what is called the "investment pyramid"

Figure 6.1:
Traditional Investment
Risk-Reward
Pyramid

RISK

REWARD

(5)
HIGHEST
RISK/HIGHEST
REWARD

(4) HIGHER RISK/
HIGHER REWARD

(3) MODERATE RISK/
MODERATE REWARD

(2) LOW RISK/
MODERATE REWARD

(1) LOW RISK/LOW REWARD

to explain the world of investment products and their risks. **Figure 6.1** shows one such investment pyramid.

The essence of these pyramids is to illustrate that if you want a high rate of return, you must take high risk and choose the investments at the top of the pyramid. If you seek low risk, you should select the investments at the bottom of the pyramid and be content to receive a low return. This type of pyramid may lead to financial trouble for some investors. No one wants to be at the bottom of the pile, so they take the chance and choose those investments at the middle or top of the pyramid.

In reality, the more risk you take, and the longer you take it, the more likely it is that a loss will occur. It is not the goal of investing to lose money but to grow it. When people do lose money, some financial advisors are quick to point out that the consumer is at fault for choosing an investment that was high up on the pyramid, and the investor should have known that there was a high degree of risk.

If you happen to see one of these pyramids, understand that you are only looking at a theory and not a working model that may be appropriate for use in choosing financial products. **The purpose of investing is to build and grow wealth, not to lose it. The purpose is not to take high risk without a defensive strategy to protect your money from loss.**

If the purpose of investing were to take a high risk to receive a high reward, then it would be called gambling and not investing. You can receive a 100 percent rate of return at a roulette wheel in a casino in Las Vegas in less than one minute, without expenses, fees, charges, or commissions, and with little complexity. Although this is true, the chance of loss is extremely high, and this is why they build billion-dollar casinos. Few people would use roulette as their long-term investing plan for retirement or college education money for their children.

Instead of the look-at-the-past-performance method or the investment-pyramid approach, people need to have a more sensible alternative. **The real goal of investing should be the antithesis of gambling and taking high risk. The goal should be to seek a high rate of return with low or no risk. That would require a more scientific approach to investing. It would take strategic thinking, a coordinated effort, certain assets, and certain advisors to make it work.** The more scientific approach should not depend on a single financial product's performance, but rather on an overall coordinated strategy that utilizes integrated products, combined with the motion of money.

Your Wealth as a Symphony

I like to explain this strategy by comparing a one-man band to an orchestra with a conductor. They both play music, but the symphony is much more expert and the sound of much higher quality.

Unfortunately, many financial advisors today are trying to sell you on one instrument rather than the symphony. They are not trained in conducting all of the financial instruments into one beautiful sound of efficiency and effectiveness. Financial strategies have to do with coordinating financial instruments to work together harmoniously for peak performance.

What financial instruments should you buy: stocks, bonds, mutual funds, variable annuities, commodities, tax shelters, real estate, racehorses, rare coins, gold, silver, futures, an IPO, or any of the hundreds of investment choices? If any person really knew which single financial investment would lead to guaranteed wealth, he would be too busy making millions of dollars every year for himself to spend time advising you. Today, most financial planners that I see are selling financial instruments rather than coordinating and integrating them to create a holistic plan that performs properly for their clients.

Where do you go to get a financial symphony? To a financial conductor versed in the Lifetime Economic Acceleration Process (LEAP). LEAP practitioners are like orchestra conductors. They are educated and trained in how to fine-tune financial products, coordinate them, integrate them, and balance your financial model for asset protection, the potential for higher-yield savings, growth, and less income taxes. They use an econometric model called the Protection, Savings, and Growth (PS&G) Model to help your money gain a higher potential for performance, efficiency, and effectiveness in reaching your desired outcomes.

Another important principle that you should know and understand about investing is: Any financial product that accumulates, compounds, reinvests, and fluctuates up and down can only grow as fast as its "internal rate of return." Whatever it earns is what you will get. It does not have any defensive strategies against taxes, inflation, expenses, fees, and charges. After these factors are considered and calculated, the result, or net rate of return on the investment, is called the "external rate of return." And eventually, such a financial investment will be left to heirs and the result of what they get is called the overall "eternal rate of return."

Every financial product has an internal, an external, and an eternal rate of return. **Most people concentrate on the internal rate of return, while they ignore the more important rates of return—the external and eternal ones. Without a financial conductor, the internal, external, and eternal rates of return on every financial asset you own may be seriously reduced in value.**

People at Work and Dollars at Work

There are two ways to make money. The first way is through work and employment. This is what I call "people at work." The second way is through savings and investments that serve to earn money for you. This is what I call "dollars at work."

When most people think of putting dollars to work to build wealth, they think only in linear terms. This is mathematical thinking and, as I have pointed out before, it is incorrect because money is not math, and math is not money. Simply growing your wealth arithmetically may only be an illusion since that wealth is going to be eroded constantly over time.

Even if your investments work out successfully and earn a high rate of return in the long run, that does not mean you have successfully overcome the eroding factors and have made money. In reality, although it may look good on paper and you feel that you have made money (and in nominal terms you may have), you may have actually "lost" money in real terms.

This real-loss concept is not obvious to many people because it is often hidden from you. It lies in the opportunities you gave up by not coordinating your money. Most people will lose millions of dollars in financial opportunity over their lifetime without ever knowing it happened to them. Losing financial potential can be as bad as losing money directly, because in most cases it is a large loss. For every dollar you lose or waste, there is always a multiplier of lost opportunity.

LOSING MONEY IS NOT VERY HARD TO DO

Let's say that ten years ago you invested $20,000 in a mutual fund, and the investment has had an annual rate of return of 8 percent. Did you make money on the investment? The answer most people would give is: "Yes, I did." But the real answer is: No, you probably did not.

First, the investment was taxable, and your combined federal and state income tax rate was between 15 percent and 40 percent. So your 8 percent annual growth rate of return was actually somewhere between

4.8 percent and 6.8 percent after taxes.

Second, inflation ran an average of about 3 percent per year. So your real rate of return was now reduced to somewhere between a low of 1.8 percent and a high of 3.8 percent after taxes and inflation.

Third, changes in technology and planned obsolescence combined to erode the value of your money by another 3 percent per year, unless you are not keeping up to date with the standard of living. This means that your net annual rate of return is somewhere between -1.8 percent and 0.8 percent.

But that is still not all. The example assumed that your 8 percent rate of return was constant, year after year. Markets don't work like that, even though many financial advisors still use the average-annual-rate-of-return method to illustrate their plans. Using an average annual rate of return may mislead you into thinking that you made more money than you actually did. An average annual rate of return does not mean a constant annual rate of return. If you started with a $100,000 investment and have a 20 percent gain in the first year and a 20 percent loss in the second year, your average annual rate of return (ROR) is 0 percent. That makes it look as if you are even and have not lost any money. But that is not the case. You have actually lost $4,000. After the first year, you had $120,000 because your investment grew by 20 percent. But then the market went down in the second year by 20 percent. Take 20 percent of $120,000 and you get a decline of $24,000. You are left with $96,000, or a $4,000 loss.

Let's see if the reverse is true. Say your $100,000 went down by 20 percent in the first year and then went up by 20 percent in the second year. Does this mean that you broke even? No, it does not—it loses too. At the end of the first year, your investment was only worth $80,000. Then in the second year, your investment went up by 20 percent. But 20 percent of $80,000 is only $16,000. So all you have at the end of the second year is $96,000—again a loss of $4,000.

Yet when the investor looks at the advertising regarding his investment in the newspaper, he sees that this investment was down 20 percent in year 1 and up 20 percent in year 2 and concludes that he is even.

Trying to build wealth through simple linear investing in taxable investments is like walking on a treadmill. You walk and walk and walk, but given the eroding factors working against you, you may not actually get anywhere. As I've mentioned in this book over and over again, the key to building wealth is to have your money moving so that it can perform more than one task. Let me explain how it works.

I know that some people feel uncomfortable with military metaphors, but I feel it can be appropriate here. You are really at war against the eroding factors of taxation, inflation, market fluctuation, interest-rate fluctuation, technological change, planned obsolescence, fees, charges, and a host of other factors. If you win, you become wealthy, and when you die you will be able to leave a financial legacy to your family and/or to charitable institutions you feel are important. If you lose the financial battles, you will not become wealthy, and when you die you will leave little if any legacy.

USE MONEY WEAPONS EFFECTIVELY

Now think of your money as weaponry in this war. The more you can get your money to do for you, the more powerful your money-weapon is in the battle against the eroding factors. **Figure 6.2** shows the difference in magnitude among money weapons that can perform certain tasks.

Figure 6.2: The Weaponry of Investment

1.	TAXABLE INVESTMENTS	= KNIFE
2.	TAX-DEFERRED INVESTMENTS	= GUN
3.	TAX-FREE INVESTMENTS	= BAZOOKA
4.	TAX-FREE AND TAX-DEDUCTIBLE	= TANK
5.	TAX-FREE, TAX-DEDUCTIBLE, AND TAX CREDIT	= BOMB

Which of these weapons would you choose in battling the eroding factors? Keep in mind that the eroding factors are relentless, formidable, and always present. If you choose a knife or a gun, you will lose the war and be overcome by the eroding factors. Yet both of those weapons have a purpose and may be important in short-term battles.

If you choose a bazooka, you may win more battles but will probably still lose the war. Yet you need to have some bazookas because there are times when they will be invaluable.

What you really need to win the big war are tanks and bombs. You need to throw the heavy artillery at the enemy, the eroding factors. But tanks and bombs must be used strategically and be protected from the enemy's defenses.

What financial products fall into these categories? You need to pick the right weapons and in the right combination. That is not easy to do.

But when you have good leadership helping you along the way, the task becomes much easier.

Most people who invest are enthralled with winning battles while they may be in fact losing the war. They focus on the battle of saving for their children's college education, the battle of saving for retirement, the income-tax battle, the high-yield battle, and the high-rate-of-return battle. All of these battles take your eye off the war. Some financial advisors call battles "needs" and "goals." The financial plan is based on winning battles, but will more often than not lose the war.

If you want to win a battle of income taxes, you may choose tax-deferred investments. The chart above shows that they are only guns. They cannot win the big war by themselves. Tax-deferred investments need the other armaments to help them win the war. Postponing the enemy by pushing them back may win the battle, but now the enemy of income taxes is consolidating and getting stronger and stronger and waiting to make their move and come down on you all at once. You will lose the war because you were not ready for them. The feel-good approach to dealing with income taxes by only deferring them is like replaying Custer's Last Stand.

By only delaying taxes, you allow the eroding factors to set their sights on the pile of money that is accumulating, waiting to be plundered. The tax bill will be paid someday, and there is no guarantee that you will save on taxes or be in a lower tax bracket. Inflation is having a field day; planned obsolescence and technological change are also eroding your purchasing power. The estate tax is looming over your pile of money as well, and interest and market fluctuations may take their share at any time too. The rigid tax-deferral approach without tanks and bombs for support is doomed.

Why do most people fall into these financial traps? Like most other things in life, a lack of knowledge is the main reason. But there is another reason. The philosophy of needs or goal planning trains people to focus on only one need at a time. They do not see their lives as being holistic. By establishing needs and goals and developing plans to meet them, financial advisors take the client off the desired course of winning the war. When money is dispersed in many directions, it loses its power. **You have heard the old saying "Divide and we will conquer." If your money is divided up into trying to win a battle here and a battle there, it will lose all of its power and be conquered. Let me explain this most important concept.**

DIVIDED AND CONQUERED

If you only have so much money to save or invest, by diversifying you actually weaken your position and the ability to build wealth effectively. You are allowing your wealth to be divided. And when it is divided, it can be conquered.

The reason people diversify is to protect themselves against major losses. But in reality, the more you spread, the greater the chance of experiencing a loss. If you have $100,000 and you invest it in one stock, you can either make a gain or a loss. The gain could be large, but so could the loss. By taking that same $100,000 and diversifying into ten stocks, your chance of losing all of your money becomes smaller, but the chance of experiencing a loss within the portfolio becomes greater. The chance of making more money by diversifying than investing in a single stock is actually significantly lower, but the chance of losing less money is significantly higher.

Diversification is one of those overrated investment strategies. That is not to say that it does not have a purpose and should not be used, because I think that it should be used when appropriate to fight battles. Every proponent of diversification speaks of averages. On average, you will be okay, they claim. You will have some losers but some winners to balance it out.

I don't know about you, but I personally do not like to have any losers when it comes to my money. I like winners, and I like being in control of my money to win the battles and the war. Diversification—dividing up your resources—can be dangerous if there is not a game plan to win the war. Diversification is a strategy, not a goal.

One day I was at a casino in Las Vegas and I was watching a player at roulette. He placed a $1 chip on 30 different numbers, 1 through 30. Now that's diversification. He would win $34 when any number came up. That is a $4 gain. He did this three times and was elated that one of his numbers came up, even though he only won $4 each time. But when double zero (00) came up on the fourth spin, he lost all $30. Small gains with a big loss don't make it. That is what occurs for many people in the financial world. They make small gains, and then when the market drops, a big loss occurs.

Four Rules for Successful Investing

In this chapter, I've explained that the right question to ask about investing is not "Where should I put my money?" but rather "How should I use my money?" Which financial products to own are not as important as how to use them once you have acquired them. There are four rules for successful investing that I have established.

RULE #1: Understand the eroding factors.
First, you need to understand that there is a problem out there in a world that is anxiously waiting to get at your money. It is not a level playing field. Eroding factors are powerful and determined forces. The more money you make, the more they can see and get from you. The goal should not just be to amass dollars like on a scoreboard. It should be to multiply them and keep them moving and out of sight. Your first thought about investing should be to build a defense. What is the purpose of building an offense if the enemy will come down and wipe you out? Know thy enemies, and make friends with them so that they do not complicate your life.

RULE #2: Choose financial products that will help defend against and counteract the eroding factors.
When selecting a financial product, do not choose it based on a short-term or long-term singular need or objective. You should select products that win the long-term war by minimizing the eroding factors while still providing dollars for all of your lifetime needs and objectives. Certain products have a dual purpose of offense and defense and are mobile to meet changing circumstances.

RULE #3: Avoid excessive fees or charges whenever possible.
I can't stress this enough. Fees are not only an immediate cost, but the money spent on fees becomes a large lost-opportunity cost into the future. The eroding factors of taxes, inflation, and market fluctuation are difficult enough to overcome without adding another cost of fees to your pile of eroding factors.

The lost-opportunity cost on fees can be quite large. If you avoid fees and invest that money yourself, many of your financial needs and goals could be easily met. You must assess the value of the fee as compared to the lost-opportunity cost. I saw a new client who had paid a financial advisor a $15,000 fee two years earlier to do a complete financial plan for him. Two years later, the client was down $30,000 in his investments and the plan design assumptions were already outmoded. When I showed the client that he will lose $1,760,000 over his expected lifetime just based on that one fee, he began to understand how damaging ongoing fees can be.

RULE #4: Have a money strategy rather than just a product purchase.

Without a coherent money strategy for your investment products, you are not going to be able to maximize your financial opportunities. How the motion of money creates additional dollars and protection against the eroding factors is key to a sound financial wealth-building process. This motion of money is called "economic acceleration."

The ability to use your money over and over again and receive a multiplier effect of benefits is the key to sound investing. It makes all the sense in the world, yet you will not see it explained in the financial literature other than in this book and in LEAP literature. Economic acceleration is the integrated and coordinated movement of money that allows your money to have more uses and helps you save taxes, avoid lost-opportunity costs, have more protection, and grow additional wealth potential.

Mutual Funds as a Taxable Investment

Choosing mutual funds for a taxable investment account and letting the dividends and capital gains be reinvested is perhaps the best example of investing without a money strategy. Since mutual funds are among the most popular ways the public invests, it is important for me to touch on them here. I have nothing against mutual funds or any other investment product. As I have said previously in the book, it is not the product that counts, it is what you do with it once you own it that is the paradigm for successful wealth building. I own some mutual funds myself, but I use them intelligently, making them produce rather than letting them sit while the eroding factors continue to do their damage on them.

What do most people do with the income from their mutual funds? They have their dividends and capital gains reinvested. They could have chosen to receive this money in cash, but instead they have decided to reinvest it back into the fund. Do they know why? Do they have a legitimate reason? Or do they just do it because it sounds good to have the money reinvested? Or was it at the advice of the mutual fund representative? In any event, reinvestment of dividends and capital gains may not be the best choice for these dollars. Why, you might ask.

Similar to the discussion on compound interest, when dividends and capital gains are reinvested, there are taxes owed on the account's dividend and capital gains distributions even if they have been reinvested. When you see a mountain chart of a mutual fund in sales literature, it does not show the taxes that were paid out of pocket each year. It also does not show the lost earnings on the money paid in taxes over the chart's time frame. Inflation is not shown either, nor is the effect of the estate tax, liability, disability, or death on the fund. All that is shown is the value of the fund over time. The real value of a fund is the difference between the cost to acquire it and the value of the money when you go to spend it.

A taxable mutual fund getting an average annual rate of return of 10 percent every single year without fail for thirty years may seem like a good investment. Most people would sign up for such a program. But in reality, it may hardly make you any money at all. **Figure 6.3** illustrates this fact. It supposes an initial investment of $25,000, with a 10 percent annual rate of return for thirty years. It further assumes that all dividends and capital gains have been reinvested, and that no withdrawals from the account have occurred. Additionally, it assumes that there is a 35 percent marginal income tax bracket and a 15 percent capital gains tax bracket, and that inflation is constant at 3 percent per year. How did it fare?

As you can see, the value of the original $25,000 investment grew over thirty years to $436,000. It sounds very impressive, doesn't it? But the tax and lost-opportunity costs on tax take $123,636. And what did the other eroding factor of inflation do to the fund? Inflation reduced the value by another $183,817. After you subtract out the original principal of $25,000 and the long-term capital gains tax of $24,674, the total gain is only $89,108, or a rate of return of 4.33 percent. Then there are other costs to be considered as well, such as fees, expenses, and charges.

Keep in mind that this fund earned 10 percent each and every year without fail and still may not have made more than an average savings rate. What is the problem? The problem is not the mutual fund—after all, it did achieve a 10 percent annual rate of return. The problem is that the money was left to compound or reinvest without a strategy to protect it from the eroding factors of taxation, lost-opportunity cost, inflation, and more. The eroding factors got the largest share of the money. What are

Figure 6.3: $25,000 Mutual Fund Investment, with Gains and Costs

YEAR	S.T. CG	TAX & L.O.C.	DIV. & CG	TAX & L.O.C.	UNREAL. CG	TOTAL VALUE
1	750	(1,736)	750	(744)	1,000	27,500
2	825	(1,793)	825	(769)	1,100	30,250
3	908	(1,852)	908	(794)	1,210	33,275
4	998	(1,913)	998	(820)	1,331	36,603
5	1,098	(1,976)	1,098	(847)	1,464	40,263
6	1,208	(2,041)	1,208	(875)	1,611	44,289
7	1,329	(2,108)	1,329	(903)	1,772	48,718
8	1,462	(2,177)	1.462	(933)	1,949	53,590
9	1,608	(2,249)	1,608	(964)	2,144	58,949
10	1,768	(2,323)	1,768	(995)	2,358	64,844
11	1,945	(2,399)	1,945	(1,028)	2,594	71,328
12	2,140	(2,478)	2,140	(1,062)	2,853	78,461
13	2,354	(2,559)	2,354	(1,097)	3,138	86,307
14	2,589	(2,643)	2,589	(1,113)	3,452	94,937
15	2,848	(2,730)	2,848	(1,170)	3,797	104,431
16	3,133	(2,820)	3,133	(1,209)	4,177	114,874
17	3,446	(2,913)	3,446	(1,248)	4,595	126,362
18	3,791	(3,008)	3,791	(1,289)	5,054	138,998
19	4,170	(3,107)	4,170	(1,332)	5,560	152,898
20	4,587	(3,209)	4,587	(1,375)	6,116	168,187
21	5,046	(3,315)	5,046	(1,421)	6,727	185,006
22	5,550	(3,424)	5,550	(1,467)	7,400	203,507
23	6,105	(3,536)	6,105	(1,516)	8,140	223,858
24	6,716	(3,653)	6,716	(1,565)	8,954	246,243
25	7,387	(3,773)	7,387	(1,617)	9,850	270,868
26	8,126	(3,897)	8,126	(1,670)	10,835	297,954
27	8,939	(4,025)	8,939	(1,725)	11,918	327,750
28	9,832	(4,157)	9,832	(1,782)	13,110	360,525
29	10,816	(4,294)	10,816	(1,840)	14,421	396,577
30	11,897	(4,435)	11,897	(1,901)	15,863	436,235
TOTAL	123,371	(86,545)	123,371	(37,091)	164,494	436,235

LONG TERM C.G. TAX	(24,674)
TOTAL COMP. TAX & L.O.C.	(123,636)
INFLATION	(183,817)
ORIGINAL PRINCIPAL	(25,000)
TOTAL GAIN	89,108

the eroding factors? Government (taxes), financial institutions (charges and expenses), corporations (inflation), and possibly a financial planner (fees). They took a large portion of the money, and the account holder had what was left. The fund was also vulnerable to a down market; money could have been lost at any time. By using the reinvestment strategy, the account holder had no other benefits such as disability, life, health, lawsuit, or estate protection.

What we can determine is that holding a mutual fund for the long term and having dividends and capital gains reinvested may appear to be a win for small battles, but it may lose the war of efficiency, effectiveness, and maximizing financial opportunity and protection.

Perhaps one should not let those dividends and capital gains be reinvested and be idle. It might be better to put those assets to good use to help fight the financial war. Remember, money in motion tends to stay in motion; money at rest tends to stay at rest and will erode over time.

Another point to consider is that since taxes are levied on the fund each year, you could wind up paying taxes on money that is no longer in the fund if the fund goes down in value. This happened in 2000-2002 to many people who owned high-tech funds in the 1990s.

Funds are also vulnerable to lawsuits. Your creditors have first crack at them in a case where you are liable for an accident that caused injury to someone else. The fund is also taxable as part of your estate at the time of your death, so the government is looking to get more from these assets, even though it has already taxed them heavily during the accumulation process.

Once again, I am not picking on mutual funds. I like mutual funds, and as I said earlier I own some of them myself. It is how the mutual funds are owned, when they are purchased, how long they are held, and what protection devices are applied to them that is paramount to their strategic use.

KEY POINTS
- **Your goal should be to have a high rate of return with low risk.**
- **Don't just win financial battles while losing the financial war.**
- **Have a money offense and defense and avoid one-dimensional financial-product strategies.**

CHAPTER 7

Casualty Insurance

In feudal times, families built strong castles made of stone with high walls and moats to protect themselves from predators. They had no insurance companies to protect their personal assets. We are fortunate that we have insurance companies to depend upon and do not have to build high walls and moats around our assets.

However, there are still financial predators in the world. They come in the form of such perils as fire, theft, hurricane, flood, tornado, accident, illness, lawsuit, disability, and death. These perils can have a major impact on your assets, income, and life values if you were to experience just one of them.

Insurance is one of the most important financial instruments in capitalism. It allows individuals, families, and businesses to shift certain risk away from themselves into a pool of those who agree to help each other out if a loss of assets, income, or life should occur to any member of the insurance pool. If insurance were suddenly declared illegal by the government, there would be a rebellion on the part of the public for its return. Insurance is something we all want to own, because it helps us feel secure. The proper purchase and use of insurance is one of the most important financial decisions an individual can make.

But unfortunately, once again, many people have been taught to think of insurance as a cost, a "necessary evil," or a "bad investment." They have not been educated to view insurance as part of the wealth-building process.

It would take volumes upon volumes of books to cover all aspects of such an important and complex area. However, in this chapter and the next I will give you some basic and key concepts to help you make better insurance decisions, save you money, and make insurance fun to own. This chapter will focus on casualty, liability, disability, and health insurance. The next chapter will focus on life insurance and long-term care insurance, both as stand-alone topics and as they relate to estate planning.

What Is Insurance?

I like to teach a simple definition of insurance to my students. If you keep this one definition in mind at all times, you will have a much stronger and productive insurance portfolio: *Insurance is the reimbursement for the full value of any item lost.*

Capitalists know how to use insurance effectively to protect their wealth, income, and lives. They do this by looking closely at the "economic value" of their assets, income, and life. Then they match that value to the proper level of insurance. Using insurance to merely satisfy a need or maintenance position does not cover the value of the item lost. Sound insurance planning is about insuring your assets, your income, and even your own life for their full value.

Ask yourself these questions:

- **If your home burned down in a fire,** would you want the insurance company to pay you the full value of the home, or just enough to build a smaller home to "meet your needs"?
- **If your car were stolen,** would you want the full value of the car to be replaced, or would you want to receive just enough money to buy a smaller, less expensive car that "meets your needs"?
- **If you became disabled and could not work,** would you want your full income replaced or just a lesser amount based on what you "need" to live?
- **If you were to die prematurely,** would you want your family to receive your full annual income, as if you were alive, or would you want them to receive just what they "need" to get by and not a penny more?

I hope your answer to each of these questions was that you want the full replacement value, and not a lesser amount that represents a perceived "need" if any of these perils befall you and your family. The most important concept I teach my students is that when a person buys insurance, he or she is buying a way of life that will occur if one of the perils happens.

Too many times I have seen people with substantially less coverage than full replacement value. When I ask why they have such a meager amount of insurance, some of the answers I get are, "That is all that I can afford," or "I don't know, it sounded good," or "I don't like insurance and I am trying to save on premium dollars."

What these well-meaning and often very intelligent people fail to realize is that their decision regarding insurance will come back to haunt them if one of the perils occurs. They will have cheated themselves and their family at the worst possible moment in their lives.

The focus of an insurance-buying decision should not be on premium cost, but should always be on obtaining full-replacement-value coverage. Rather than seeking out the cheapest policy (which often provides the fewest benefits, and hence the least value), you should seek to insure for the full value of the asset, income, or life you are trying to protect. When discussing any form of insurance, first imagine the peril occurring in your life, then select the coverage that will make your life happy or complete if that peril actually occurred. See it in your mind, feel what it would be like both now and in the future. Remember, no one complains when the insurance company pays off a claim for full value rather than a smaller amount.

Once that amount has been ascertained, then the cost and how to pay for it comes into play. But never settle for less coverage than what you would want to have if the peril did occur.

Premium Versus Coverage

As I just stated, full-value coverage is far more important than premium considerations. In an ideal world, you would always have full-value coverage, regardless of the premium cost. But we live in a world where the money for premiums is important and may be hard to come by or even scarce in your household. How much to pay and the type of insurance policy to buy is a very complex and difficult subject. Experts in the financial services industry disagree with one another on this subject; so how are you to make the correct decision?

Let me give you some general rules you can follow to make your decisions easier:

1. **Don't seek to cover the first dollar of loss**, but insure against the larger catastrophe.
2. **Don't cover risks** that will have little impact on your wealth, happiness, or success.
3. **Have an insurance expert on your side to help you** design the insurance policies suitable for your financial life situation.
4. **Have other people pay for your premiums,** or lower or even recapture their cost over time.

Obviously, it is item #4 that is the least understood and the most difficult to accomplish. But a true insurance expert can show you how to recapture premium costs and not have a premium cost, or find ways for other people to pay the premium. Anyone can sell you a policy, but few people have the ability to help you create an efficient and effective insurance portfolio. A LEAP practitioner is trained to provide you with this type of insurance planning.

Another important question I ask my clients regarding insurance is as follows:

"If you could acquire the maximum amount of insurance at no additional out-of-pocket outlay, what would prevent you from owning the best policy with the most coverage?" The answer I always get is, "Nothing, I would want to own the best policy with the highest coverage if I had no additional premium outlay to own it."

Well, that's where you should start. Never start with the lowest-premium policy, because it usually has the worst coverage and the worst benefits. You will lose some way or other. You should always start with the best and see if it can be acquired at no or little additional premium outlay to you by working with an expert, not just an insurance salesperson or the insurance company.

Remember the four rules of financial institutions: They want your money; they want to get your money systematically; they want to keep it for a long period of time; and they want to pay you back as little as possible when you want it. Well, insurance companies are financial institutions too. No insurance company is in the business of giving money away. They are in the business of providing benefits, paying claims, and making a profit for their investors as well.

Recognize that profits are an important part of insurance companies' ability to provide a service. You should want them to make a profit, otherwise there would be no insurance and we would all be in trouble financially.

Suppose there are two insurance companies offering the same coverage of $1 million if a particular peril occurs. One company offers the coverage at a premium of $1,500 and the other is charging $350. At first glance, you might say the decision is easy. You buy the policy that has a premium of $350.

Not so fast. You must ask yourself why that company is offering the same coverage at a substantially lower premium. Will the coverage run out? Are there exclusions to the coverage? Does the premium increase over time? Does the policy have benefits that are less than the other policy? The answers to all these questions, and more, must be ascertained before a good decision can be made. That is what makes insurance difficult to purchase; there are so many differences among the policies offered.

You must remember that premium should rarely be the deciding factor. It is unfortunate to see so many people base their insurance-buying decisions on premium; they no doubt wind up in trouble someday because of that decision. The old saying "you get what you pay for" is so true in the insurance marketplace.

Types of Insurance

Let's start with the types of insurance policies. You have already purchased many of these types of policies and they should be familiar to you. But I hope to shed some light on them so you can strengthen your insurance portfolio.

Insurance for individuals and households falls into one of six categories:

- **Casualty**
- **Liability**
- **Disability**
- **Health**
- **Life**
- **Long-Term Care**

CASUALTY INSURANCE

The two most common types of casualty insurance held by individuals are auto and home insurance. Auto insurance and home insurance (whether you are a renter, an owner of a single-family home, or an owner of a home in a common-ownership association such as a condominium) provide insurance protection for your home or auto, as well as your personal property, against many perils, as stated in the policy.

As a general rule, you should keep the deductible on casualty policies as high as you can afford. The deductible is the amount you will have to pay out of pocket before the insurance company pays for the rest of any damage claim. As a rule, the higher the deductible, the lower the premium.

Although you pay a lower premium for a high deductible, you will be paying for the gap underneath the deductible if a peril occurs. If that would be a financial burden, then you need a lower deductible to narrow the gap. The idea of having a higher deductible is that over time you save on premiums, and those premium savings can then be used to pay for the gap portion in the future if a peril occurred. If a peril doesn't occur, you saved money. Of course, if you have frequent claims, a higher deductible can cost more money over time. But the truth is that the vast majority of people have so few claims that they can save money by raising their deductibles, reducing their premiums, and "self-insuring" the gap in coverage.

Deductibles on auto insurance only pertain to damage caused by you or if someone hits your car and leaves the scene. This is called collision insurance. Many people today carry at least a $250 deductible on collision. Some can afford a $500 deductible, a $1,000 deductible or even a $2,000 deductible. In most instances, if another driver hits your car, you receive payment for the damage from his or her insurance company.

For theft, you should cover the actual value of the car. If your car is in an accident with someone who is driving without insurance, your uninsured motorist feature covers that event. Most states now include mandatory coverage on your policy for uninsured motorist coverage.

With regard to home insurance coverage, the same kind of thinking related to deductibles should apply. Since your home insurance policy covers you anywhere in the world, it is more comprehensive than auto insurance, which is only vehicle related. I like to see the deductible for home insurance the same as the auto policy deductible.

Renters need only insure their own property, not the landlord's property. Owners of condominium or cooperative units need to check with their association to see what is covered by the association's insurance and what needs to be covered by the individual (e.g., in a multistory building, is the association or the unit owner responsible for covering damage from leaks in the plumbing of another unit that causes damage to the unit owner's property).

Increasing deductibles can reduce the cost of insurance if there are, say, two cars and a home, by literally hundreds, if not thousands, of dollars each year. The money saved from one form of insurance can then be applied toward needed insurance coverage in other areas.

You should always have photos and sales receipts of most of your items not separately insured. This documentation should be stored out of the home in case the home is destroyed by fire, flood, hurricane, tornado, etc.

You should seek out the advice of a licensed casualty broker to explain all of your options and coverage, as well as premiums. No general rules in this section should be relied upon as specific information in your own personal financial situation without the advice of an expert casualty agent.

LIABILITY INSURANCE

Liability insurance is one of the most important forms of insurance to protect all of your assets and income. You are exposed to potential liability for many events—whether intentional or unintentional—such as an auto accident you cause, if your dog bites someone, a drowning in your swimming pool, a fight, someone tripping on your icy walkway, etc. You need to protect your assets and income from such potential liabilities. All the best financial planning and careful money management can be torn asunder with one lawsuit. It can happen at any time, to anyone. You must be prepared.

There are basically three types of liability coverage to protect yourself and your assets from this peril. You can use the liability coverage in your auto policy or your home insurance policy, or you can acquire a general liability policy or an excess liability policy. Your auto policy and home insurance policy have liability coverage amounts that you can choose from. Most insurance companies sell auto policies with maximum liability coverage of $300,000 per individual if you injure someone else, and $500,000 per accident if more than one individual claims damages. Most home insurance policies have maximum liability protection of $500,000. If the maximum liability amounts on your auto and home insurance policies do not protect all of your assets, it then becomes necessary to purchase a separate liability policy, often known as an "umbrella policy."

A liability umbrella policy usually provides a minimum of $1 million in "excess" liability coverage, above what your auto or home policy covers, and you can purchase umbrellas for up to $10 million or more. When calculating if you need an umbrella, take into account your income as well as your assets (a legal judgment for more than your assets can include orders that you pay more out of your continuing income). Liability protection protects your assets against claims for any negligent act you may commit that damages someone else's property, or injures or kills someone.

Once again, you should seek out the advice of a licensed casualty broker to explain all of your options and coverage, as well as premiums. No general rules in this section should be relied upon as specific information in your own personal financial situation without the advice of an expert casualty agent.

HEALTH INSURANCE

The world of health insurance is constantly changing. Most families do have some form of health insurance. Most people have either a company-sponsored health insurance plan through their employer, government-sponsored insurance, or their own private health insurance coverage.

Health care costs are continuing to rise more rapidly than the general inflation rate because of new technology, more and more frequent use of prescription drugs, and the fact that people are living longer and need more health care services of all kinds. By 2025, it is estimated by those who follow census data trends that in Canada and the United States, those older than 85 will be the fastest-growing segment of the population. You can guess what that will do to health care costs.

For those who have private coverage, I believe you should consider raising your deductible the same way you do for auto and home insurance. Many people will use at least a portion of their health insurance deductible each year; in other words, the deductible should be considered as an annual expense along with the premium. If you don't use the entire deductible, you have in effect "saved" money. In addition, I believe everyone should carry a major medical maximum of at least $1 million in lifetime benefits.

The subject of health insurance is a vast and expansive arena, with politicians, insurance companies, health care providers such as doctors and hospitals, and drug companies all in the fray to design a better and more comprehensive approach. The outlook is good for resolution as long as the public understands that quality health care is as important, if not more important, than just having coverage for everyone. If everyone has coverage and our quality of health care declines because of it, then we have all failed. We need to have coverage available for those who want it, but must maintain high-quality health care for those who have it.

DISABILITY INSURANCE

If you become disabled, whether by accident or illness, the reason for having disability insurance is obvious. If you lose your income, it will cause financial hardship on top of emotional hardship. If you do not have financial assets that are sufficient to live on for the rest of your life, you are in need of disability insurance.

I ask my clients the following question: "If you went to work tomorrow and your employer cut your salary in half, what would you do?" They often say, "I would quit and find another job, because I couldn't live on that salary."

That's right, you couldn't live on that salary—at least not in the way you want to live. I then explain that when you become disabled, it is like your employer cutting your salary in half, or even worse. You can't quit a disability. You can't find another job. You have no choice; you need to have disability insurance to replace the income lost to you and your family. The amount of disability income should be for the full value of your lost income, not a penny less. You and your family deserve the same quality of life even if an unfortunate accident or illness were to occur.

I am appalled at the amount of disability insurance most people carry. If a disability were to occur, they would be in financial difficulty. I ask, "Why do you have so little coverage?" The answers I get most are, "I guess if I'm disabled I won't need any money," or "That is all my employer will offer," or "I can't afford disability insurance; it is too expensive."

These are not legitimate reasons to go without full protection. You only have one life to live, and you better plan to live it in the best manner possible. You actually need more income when you are disabled. Whatever your employer provides can be supplemented in the private arena, and it is not expensive when you know how to acquire it with little or no additional out-of-pocket outlay.

The best form of disability insurance is to have your own private policy. Group disability or association disability policies have many disadvantages that are often not known or are overlooked.

Actually, disability insurance provided by an employer may not be a fringe benefit, but instead a fringe problem.

- **First,** the amount of coverage may be tied to your base salary only, and not include your bonus.
- **Second,** the definition of disability may be very weak and you may not qualify for coverage if you can perform a lower-paying job.
- **Third,** the coverage may be level-income and not rise each year with inflation.
- **Fourth,** the coverage may stop at age 65, or sooner; since you were unable to save for retirement and lost your retirement plan when you became disabled, you will have a real financial problem then.
- **Fifth,** the coverage most likely is integrated with government benefits; that means whatever you receive from any government-sponsored program will be subtracted from the monthly benefit you receive from the disability insurance.
- **Sixth,** the disability income may be taxable as if it were earned income.
- **Seventh,** the employer-sponsored disability policy is not portable; that means that if you leave your employment for another job, or get downsized, you can't take the policy with you.

A private disability income policy can eliminate all of the disadvantages of group or association coverage. Here are my recommendations:

1. **Buy a private policy or wrap-around group policy**, whenever you can, while you are insurable and young.
2. **Insure yourself** for 80 percent of your gross income.
3. **Have a relatively long waiting period.** You can perhaps find ways to have income during the waiting period. Having a long waiting period lowers your premium and makes the policy more affordable. You can use the earnings on your assets and other resources to live on, and many companies allow you to bank sick days and accumulate vacation days for such times.
4. **Have a strong definition of disability** (it should be your "own occupation").
5. **Reduce or eliminate disability coverage** as your assets and

wealth grow to sufficient levels to provide the need for income during a time of disability.

6. **Do not overlook the importance of the disability** "waiver-of-premium" rider on your life insurance policies. These riders and their benefits can be a very helpful addition to your disability benefit planning.

No matter how you become disabled, whether through accident or illness, you deserve to live a life of dignity and continue to live a complete life. Your family also depends on the quality of your disability coverage. Make sure that you have the right amount of coverage and coordinate it with the other assets of Social Security, pensions, life insurance, and individually owned assets.

KEY POINTS
- Insure for full value, not need.
- Increase deductibles if you can afford it.
- Start with the best policy and see if it can be acquired before you settle for less.

CHAPTER 8

Life Insurance, Long-Term Care Insurance, and Estate Planning

Everyone should own life insurance. Everyone has a value, and anything of value should be insured against loss. Every adult is an asset, whether he or she owns a business, works for someone else, cares for family members, cares for the home, or does a combination of two or more things. The value an individual produces in his or her role in life is an asset and should be insured.

You may read in the financial media many articles about life insurance and how to determine the "need" for it. Many financial writers have stated that you may not need any life insurance, especially if you are "only a housewife." The best advice I can give to you is to completely ignore them. They do not know the harm that they do to people by giving such bad advice.

It is unfortunate that most life insurance advisors have been improperly trained; they have been trained to determine the amount of insurance a person should own by using what is called a "needs analysis" calculation. If you hear the word "need" in any conversation, or see it in any written material about life insurance, you immediately know that the person using such a term has little knowledge about life insurance and how it works.

Why do I say that "needs-analysis-type" planning is inappropriate?

I say it because no beneficiary or survivor, given the choice, would want only an amount of insurance that they supposedly "need" rather than the true value of the insured person who died. Insurance companies will insure individuals up to their true value. That amount is the most that they will offer. You can't get more than that amount, just like you can't get more home insurance than what your house is worth.

If your house burned down, you would want full value, not less. When a person dies, the beneficiary would not want less money than what the deceased was worth. Why would the beneficiary only want what was needed to make ends meet, and leave the true value of the insured for the insurance company to keep?

For instance, I ask my client, in this case a male working spouse, "If you knew you were going to die tomorrow, how much life insurance would you buy today?" The only answer that would make any sense is, "All I could get." Premium would not matter since the rate of return would be enormous in one day. If a man loves his family, he should want them to have the best and true value of his life.

What reason would there be not to get the most insurance that was available if you knew you were going to die tomorrow? Most people say, "I can't think of any reason why I wouldn't want my family to have the maximum amount available." Then I ask, "What if the maximum amount had no additional out-of-pocket outlay to you?" They typically answer, "That would be a no-brainer. I would definitely want to get the maximum amount of life insurance."

The last and perhaps the most important question is then asked: "Could you die tomorrow, and how does not knowing when you are going to die change anything?"

They finally get it. There is no logical reason why anyone would not want to have the full amount of the value of the insured. Why settle for less on your life, your most valued asset, if you would not settle for less on your home, car, jewelry, boat, office building, or any other asset you insure? **Needs analysis is inaccurate because it puts the emphasis of life insurance on the needs of the beneficiary instead of on the value of the insured.**

A good rule of thumb to use is that if you are under age 35, your economic value is approximately 20 times your gross income. If you are between age 36 and 50, your replacement value is about 15 times your gross income. If you are age 51 and over and still working, your replacement value is about 10 times your gross income. If you are retired, your replacement value is the value of your net worth.

You can acquire full-value insurance for your life at little or no additional out-of-pocket outlay over and above what you are now paying for life insurance, by using the Lifetime Economic Acceleration Process (LEAP). A LEAP practitioner can show you how to do it.

The first major misconception about life insurance is that when you buy life insurance, you are primarily buying death protection. That is totally incorrect. Anyone who proposes that does not understand life insurance. That would be like saying that the only reason to own a car is to drive to work. People buy cars for many reasons, least of which may be to go to work. They could use a bike, bus, car pool, train, or taxi.

In truth, there are many more reasons to buy life insurance than simply to provide pure death protection. When buying life insurance, you are buying love of family, love of self, financial security, suit protection, disability protection, tax savings, liquidity, collateral, guaranteed savings, increased rate of return, peace of mind, and a foundation for financial flexibility and success.

The pundits who advocate buying pure death protection—and the readers who take them to heart—will have death protection and nothing else. The only way to win that way is by dying early, and the odds are against that. A good capitalist knows how to use life insurance for more than just death protection. A good capitalist knows how to use life insurance to make his or her entire financial life a success and build wealth.

The second major misconception about life insurance is that you should only insure for the "premature death need." This is the oldest mistake in the handbook on how to buy or sell life insurance. In reality, most people will not die before they retire. Therefore, the need for "premature death protection" is not as great as the need for "ultimate death protection" and all of the other uses of life insurance while alive.

A third misconception is that you won't need life insurance later in your life. While we never want to make a claim for a car accident, hurricane, fire, disability, or other health issue, we know we are all going to die. It will happen, and the life insurance portfolio you design should be there when it happens. You can insure your value in your lifetime, which allows you to leave a public legacy and also leave money to your family.

A fourth misconception is that term-life insurance is the cheapest form of life insurance. Term-life insurance does have the lowest premium, but in reality it is the most expensive form of insurance to own. Some sales-people spend time trying to convince consumers that term life insurance is cheapest. They provide misinformation to get their point across.

They don't tell you that more than 95 percent of all term-life policies never pay a claim. They don't tell you that your real cost is not just the premium, but the earnings you could have gotten on the premium, plus the loss of the death benefit that will not be paid out. They omit the last two items.

This is not to say that term-life insurance has no place in many people's life insurance portfolio. It does, but only for a very short period of time and for a very specific purpose.

If you assume you will live past retirement age, you should want to own the life insurance policy that provides the most living benefits as well as a death benefit. That means traditional whole-life insurance should play the most prominent role in every individual's life insurance portfolio. Whole-life insurance has the most guarantees and the most living bene-fits of all forms of life insurance, and the highest overall rate of return, historically speaking.

Let me explain why.

Whole-Life Insurance: The Living Engine of Our Lives

At first glance, many people do not see the advantages of owning a whole-life policy. They see a high premium, as compared to a relatively low premium for term life insurance. But ask yourself, why would a com-pany be willing to give me $1 million of coverage for an annual premium of only $800 a year for twenty years while the same company is charging an annual premium of $12,000 for a whole-life policy? Before you answer, read on.

What costs more, a bag of gold or a bag of glass marbles?

Insurance companies know from actuarial calculations that their term-life policies will not result in many death claims. Of the millions of term-life insurance policies sold, fewer than 5 percent will result in a death benefit being paid. Most policies either expire or lapse.

The only way you can win with term-life insurance is to die young, and that is not a scenario that any of us would actually call winning. If you out-live the policy—and you most likely will—you lose, and you will lose a substantial amount of money.

Once I lay out the benefits of whole-life insurance for you, I think you'll see that it should have a place in every individual's life insurance portfolio.

- **The premium is guaranteed.** Whole-life insurance has a guaranteed level premium for the life of the policy. It does not change over time, and you never have to worry about an increase in premium due to poor health, interest rates, or stock market conditions.
- **The premium consists of a guaranteed "cash value" as well as a death benefit.** Only a small portion of the premium in a whole-life policy represents the "cost of insurance." Most of the premium consists of your savings, called cash value. So whole life is both an insurance and a savings vehicle. Term-life insurance does not have the savings feature; it only has the insurance cost. It is this savings feature that makes whole life a very important financial tool and one you should seriously consider.
- **Cash value accrues tax-advantaged.** The cash value increases, tax-free, until the policy's cash values are greater than the total premiums paid. At that point, the cash value in the policy grows on a tax-deferred basis. When death occurs, all of the policy's cash values are an income-tax-free benefit no matter how much the gain over the premiums paid.
- **The whole-life policy also pays a dividend.** Once a year, a traditional whole-life policy declares a dividend. The amount of the annual dividend from year to year is unknown, and paying the dividend is done at the discretion of the insurance company. But when the policy is sold, the company makes a projection of these dividends based upon its current financial position. Therefore, the dividend is technically not "guaranteed"; it could be higher or lower than what the company projected for that year.

  A good thing to do is to ask your life insurance agent for a complete dividend history of the company so you can see the company's past performance. Most insurance companies have paid dividends consistently for over 100 years. And keep in mind that once a dividend has been paid to you it cannot be lost or taken away; it is guaranteed to remain. That is unlike dividends on investments, which, if they are reinvested in the investment, can be lost due to future market declines.

No one can predict the future, but when it comes to whole-life-insurance dividends, they have historically been a reliable source of extra funds for individuals and families.

- **Premiums can be paid by the insurance company for you if you become disabled.** Although you must pay a small amount of extra premium for it, the disability-waiver-of-premium rider is well worth having. With this rider, should you become disabled, the insurance company will continue to pay the full premium for you. Since most of the premium is actually cash value, the cash value and any dividends/interest will continue to build up to help you meet any future savings needs, such as college education for your children or your own retirement income. Whole-life insurance is an intelligent way to meet your future financial needs and obligations should you become disabled. Whole-life insurance comes to your rescue at a time when you need it most, and when every other savings and investment product is shutting down.

  A client of mine, an attorney, became totally disabled due to multiple sclerosis at age 32. He could no longer work, and he had a wife and two small children. His pension stopped growing; his 401(k) plan stopped taking in new money; his mutual funds no longer took in any new money; and all he had for current income was a disability insurance policy that paid 60 percent of his salary. But he had a significant portfolio of whole-life insurance with disability-waiver-of-premium riders. Those policies continued to have premiums paid, and continued to accumulate cash value and dividends. When his kids reached college age, it was possible for him to use the built-up cash values and dividends to fund their tuition (I'll talk about this more in the next chapter). He and his wife have enough built up so she can retire with dignity and income. He is forever grateful that he purchased that insurance policy at a young age.

- **Whole life provides wide flexibility.** You can use your dividends in many different ways. To me, one of the best ways to use the dividends is to have them purchase additional paid-up insurance, which increases the policy's death benefit over time. This helps fight inflation, compared with the death benefit of a term policy, which remains level or even declines over time.

  But should you need to, you can also take the dividend in the form of cash each year. You can use the dividend to supplement your income, to invest, or to pay down any debt you might have. You can also use your dividend to pay the policy's premium; as time goes by, the dividend may be large enough to pay the entire premium.

- **You can borrow money from your policy.** You don't have to surrender a policy to access your cash value. The "policy loan" provision allows you to borrow up to the amount of the cash value. Unlike other kinds of loans, you never have to pay this loan back, as long as you keep paying the premium and the current interest on the loan. The loan only has to be paid off at the time of death, from the proceeds of any death benefit paid out to your beneficiaries.

  One thing I want to make clear here is that you are not borrowing your own money. Many financial writers and advisors erroneously claim that you are borrowing your own money and therefore you should not be paying any interest. This is untrue. It is not your money you are borrowing; you cannot be your own banker. When you borrow against an insurance policy's cash value, you are actually borrowing money from the insurance company and allowing the insurance company to hold your cash value intact as collateral for the loan.

- **You can also use your cash value as collateral for a bank loan.** Banks will normally loan close to 100 percent on the cash value and dividends in the account, on a favorable basis.

- **The cash value is exempt from creditors.** This is a little-known but very important benefit of whole-life insurance. In most states, life insurance cash value is not exposed to a liability judgment. Check with your insurance company to determine if this is true in your state.

In summary, when you take into account all of the benefits of growth in guaranteed cash value, declared dividends, income tax savings, avoiding costly term-insurance premiums, and the high overall rate of return over a period of time, it is very difficult to find a savings or investment vehicle that has consistently returned more money than whole-life insurance. Add to this the peace of mind and ease with which this rate of return is accomplished, and the lack of risk involved

in whole-life insurance, and it is nearly impossible to have a more effective and efficient way to build and protect your wealth.

The only significant disadvantage to whole-life insurance is that it is not a short-term financial product. Whole life is a lifelong financial product that acts as one of the pillars of your wealth-building process. The cash value does not really begin to build up until the policy has been in force for a couple of years. Whole-life insurance is definitely a long-term insurance product and should not be considered if you are making a short-term purchase.

Term Life Insurance

Term insurance has a place in many people's life insurance portfolio. It is the opposite of whole life. It builds no cash value; its death benefit stays level or declines; it is for the short term rather than the long term; and it will most likely "run out of" death benefit by lapsing or expiring. It is like sticking your thumb in a dike and holding back the water until you can afford to buy whole-life insurance.

Term insurance is often purchased because it is inexpensive. The reason it is inexpensive is that it only provides a death benefit, and only for a specified time. For this reason, it should be used only in a specific short-term need for a death benefit and not as part of a serious long-term financial plan or estate plan.

Whenever buying an individual term-insurance policy, you should always seek to buy insurance that is convertible (policies bought through groups like an employer or a professional or alumni association are rarely if ever convertible). Buying convertible term life at an early age guarantees insurability later, even if your health deteriorates. Whenever possible, you should seek to convert term life to whole-life insurance as soon as you can afford to do so.

Universal Life Insurance

Universal life is a combination of term insurance and an insurance annuity (it is sometimes described as an annuity in an insurance wrapper). Universal life typically has a lower premium than whole life, and flexibility of premium payments. This affords you more death benefit for the same premium as whole life, while allowing you to adjust your premium to suit a changing budget.

Universal life pays a straight interest rate on the cash value in the annuity portion of the policy. The interest rate changes annually or semi-annually, depending on the policy. The lack of a dividend is a disadvantage of universal life. Another disadvantage is that interest cannot be removed tax-free if you wish to take the interest in cash. Although some universal life offers a disability waiver of premium, this waiver in many cases is only on the pure protection portion of the policy, and the cash value does not increase from that point. Also, if you choose to pay a lower premium, this can reduce the ultimate death benefit and even risk policy lapse if the interest rate declines.

This is not an appropriate insurance policy to use for retirement planning, estate planning, income tax strategies, or charitable giving, because the death benefit can fluctuate and the tax benefits are not as advantageous as with whole life. Universal life should be viewed as more appropriate than term insurance as a long-term death benefit. But it is not as appropriate to use as whole-life insurance for more permanent needs.

If you think of whole life as being the luxury car, universal life as a midsize car and term-life insurance as an economy car, you will have an analogy that is useful to your understanding of the differences among these products. They offer different advantages and disadvantages, and the difference in price should not be the only factor in deciding which to purchase.

Variable Life Insurance

Like universal life, variable-life insurance is a combination of term insurance and an annuity. However, instead of a straight interest-payment annuity, with variable life you have a choice of how to invest the cash value among many different "sub accounts," which are essentially mutual funds.

This "investment" of cash value rather than "saving" of cash value offers the possibility of increasing the cash value above what a universal-life or whole-life policy could offer. But it also puts the cash value at risk. Another disadvantage is that there are no dividends, and you must borrow to get money out of the policy. If you borrow from the policy and the stock market declines at the same time, you may experience more premium "calls," or a loss of death benefits, or the policy may even lapse.

Variable life is not appropriate for retirement planning, estate planning, income-tax strategies, or charitable giving, since the growth of its cash value is not secure or guaranteed. The success of the policy is strictly a matter of chance in the markets, and you take all of the risks.

Survivorship Life Insurance (Second-to-Die)

Survivorship-life insurance (also called second-to-die insurance) is most often used as an estate-planning tool. It is most attractive for couples older than age 70 with large, illiquid estates, to avoid a forced sale of assets in order to pay estate taxes.

Survivorship life is not appropriate for those under age 55, because of the large lost-opportunity costs involved in many years of premium payments until the second spouse dies. If either of the spouses lives to age 90, the premium cost and lost-opportunity cost on the premiums paid is greater than the death benefit provided. In essence, you would have prepaid your estate tax in premiums, or even more.

Survivorship insurance has another disadvantage as well. In order for the insurance to be kept out of the estate, it must be held in a trust. The trust is irrevocable, and the premiums must be paid by the insured individual(s) by making annual allowable gifts to the trust. After the first spouse dies, the annual gift allowance is reduced, and could require a gift tax to be paid by the surviving spouse for the amount put into the trust to pay the premium. This could go on for many years, increasing the lost-opportunity costs of holding the policy.

Many of the estate-planning goals taken care of by survivorship insurance can be taken care of in other ways that do not incur these lost-opportunity costs. Therefore, survivorship life insurance should only be used sparingly, for much older couples with illiquid estates.

Settlement Options

The most critical decision you can make about any life-insurance policy or group benefit is how the proceeds should be paid to beneficiaries at your death. Should the proceeds be paid out in a single sum to a beneficiary or should it be paid out in installments?

You can arrange while you are alive to have the insurance proceeds of your insurance policies and your group-life policies paid out as you choose. All you have to do is decide which payment option is best for you and your beneficiaries in order to avoid any potential future financial problems for them.

There are five options to choose from when paying out the death-benefit proceeds from a life-insurance policy to your beneficiaries. These options are called settlement options. They are:

1. **Lump-Sum or One-Sum Option**
2. **Interest Option**
3. **Equal-Installment Option**
4. **Life-Expectancy Option**
5. **Life Insurance Trusts**

1. LUMP-SUM OR ONE-SUM OPTION

Too many people have their insurance proceeds paid out in one sum to their beneficiaries, and these proceeds may be lost due to a variety of reasons. Your beneficiary may spend all the money frivolously, invest it improperly, get defrauded, or otherwise mismanage the proceeds. The money may go to a person other than whom you intended.

Most people choose the one-sum option, not because that is what they want, but because nothing else was ever explained to them. In most cases the one-sum option is the default option on the policy if no other option is chosen.

2. INTEREST OPTION

The next settlement option is called the interest option, where the principal of the death benefit stays with the insurance company and only the interest is paid to the beneficiary. This option has great appeal since the purpose of insurance is to pay income to the beneficiary to replace the income of the insured. Also, it gives the beneficiary time to think, rather than having the money come in at a time when there is so much change or even confusion. Under this option, the beneficiary has the right to choose any other option, including one-sum, at any future time, by making a written request to the company. Another advantage of this option is that it keeps the insurance proceeds out of the hands of the beneficiary's creditors as long as it remains inside the life-insurance-policy settlement option.

3. EQUAL-INSTALLMENT OPTION

Another settlement option is an equal-installment option of a ten-, fifteen-, or twenty-year payout. Whatever the amount of the insurance proceeds of your policy, the insurance company can pay it out in equal installments over the amount of time you choose. For instance, if you have insurance benefits of $1 million, your beneficiary would receive $118,000 including interest each year for ten years; $86,500 including interest for fifteen years, or $70,751 including interest for twenty years.

4. LIFE-EXPECTANCY OPTION

There is also a life-expectancy settlement option, where the principal and interest is paid out over the beneficiary's life expectancy. Let's say the beneficiary is age 50 at the time of the insured's death, and the beneficiary's life expectancy is thirty years. The payout on a $1 million death benefit would be about $56,000 a year for the life of the beneficiary.

Settlement options are a way to assure that your beneficiary will receive the insurance proceeds the way you intended. You can protect him or her from the financial pitfalls of having the money arrive in one sum. Although one sum may be well intentioned, it often leads to financial trouble for the beneficiary. In addition, many insured people appreciate the idea of having the insurance proceeds paid out over time so they will be remembered and loved for their caring and generosity for a longer period of time.

5. LIFE INSURANCE TRUSTS

You can also have life-insurance proceeds paid in one sum to a life insurance trust drafted by an estate-planning attorney. The trust collects the proceeds and follows the instructions you have written down in the trust agreement. You select a trustee to manage the funds for the beneficiary and instruct the trustee to pay the funds to the beneficiary any way you desire, with any privileges and restrictions on the funds you choose.

Some people like to have beneficiaries qualify for the income by setting various lifestyle requirements. Only through a trust can you customize when, how, where, and what funds are to be paid, and to whom they will be paid. For this reason, life insurance trusts are often a favored mechanism when there is a large amount of insurance proceeds.

These trusts are written prior to the insured's death, and can be reviewed and modified on an annual basis. The trust is not activated until the insured dies. Your estate-planning attorney can explain all the details of ownership of such a trust.

Between all of the insurance-policy settlement options and the life insurance trust option, you can be confident that policy proceeds will be managed properly and used in the manner you want.

Long-Term Care Insurance

The big question is, do you need it?

For many of my clients, the answer is no, they do not need it. For others, the answer is most definitely that they do need it. What makes the difference?

If you have sufficient wealth, life insurance, a home you own, a pension plan, and Social Security payments, you very well may not need long-term care insurance. If you lack a strong plan in any of these areas, you need to consider purchasing long-term care insurance. It all comes down to how much money you will have accumulated by the time you need medical-assisted living.

If you have a sound retirement plan, funds that would have been used for an active retirement can be used instead to go toward the cost of medical-assisted living. There is no loss of wealth to estate beneficiaries since your retirement funds would have been depleted anyway. When you are in need of medical-assisted living, you are no longer spending money to play golf, eat at restaurants, travel, go to movies and sporting events, or buy a new car. In other words, your retirement-income planning is essentially your long-term care insurance policy.

In addition, if you have whole-life insurance in the amount of your economic replacement value, the need for long-term care insurance also diminishes greatly. The whole-life policy stays intact even if you deplete all of your other assets for medical-assisted living, allowing you to leave your beneficiaries money to replace what you have used up.

If you own a home without a mortgage, you can tap into that home for what is called a reverse mortgage. The mortgage company will pay you an income for life, tax-free, and without any out-of-pocket outlay by you. The loan accrues inside the mortgage and will be due when you die or sell the house. You can use these proceeds to help pay for any medical-assisted living costs.

Thus, if you have financial assets, a home, whole-life insurance, and a retirement-income plan, chances are that you do not need long-term care insurance. You would be better off saving the premium and investing it into your own retirement-income plan or a whole-life insurance policy.

If you do not have much in the way of assets, life insurance, a mortgage-free home, and a sound retirement plan, you are definitely a candidate for long-term care insurance. What few assets you have will be eaten up quickly, and you will not be able to afford the quality of care you would want and deserve to have. At these times, having a respectable and dignified medical-care assistance program is paramount to your quality of life and your ability to not be a burden to anyone, while maintaining the love of your family and the preservation of your wealth.

Estate Planning

An estate plan is designed to make sure your assets are conserved and distributed properly after your death. Everyone needs an estate plan. Even if you don't have an estate large enough to trigger an estate tax, an estate plan is necessary to make sure your assets go to the right people, at the right time, and with any appropriate restrictions and privileges.

There are two major objectives to any estate plan:

1. **Distribution of assets** (make sure assets go to the right person, at the right time, with the right conditions and restrictions)
2. **Conservation of assets** (avoid probate; eliminate or at least minimize income tax, estate tax, court costs, appraisal fees, and other estate-closing costs)

It is not necessary for your estate plan's design to be complex for it to meet these two objectives. In fact, overly complex estate plans can create their own problems; they are often costly to draft and difficult to manage over time. Let's delve a little more deeply into these two objectives of estate planning.

DISTRIBUTION OF ASSETS

There are a number of different ways in which you can choose to own and hold your assets. Each way of owning or holding an asset uses a different methodology to pass that asset to a beneficiary. Whenever possible, you want to own or hold assets in such a way that they can pass to a beneficiary with as little time lag, red tape, and cost as possible.

For instance, with joint ownership of property, when one owner dies, the property passes directly to the other owner, avoiding probate costs. Many couples or pairs of siblings hold property such as a home in joint ownership for this reason.

If a person owns an asset individually, at the time of death that property goes into the deceased owner's probate estate. If the person has no will, assets are divided among beneficiaries according to state intestate law. For example, in many states, one-third of the estate goes to the deceased's spouse and the other two-thirds of the estate is divided among the deceased's children.

If the person has a will, assets pass to beneficiaries according to the directives outlined in the will, assuming that there are no successful challenges to the will and its provisions. Challenges most often come from an individual who has been left out of the will. This is often a child who has had a falling-out with a parent, or a non-family member who has cared for an elderly person for many years. "Hard assets" such as cars, jewelry, antiques, art, and coins can only be passed to a specified beneficiary through a will or trust.

A will can be contested on three basic grounds:

- **The deceased was not mentally competent at the time the will was made.**
- **The deceased was under mental and/or physical duress when the will was made.**
- **The provisions of the will are grossly unfair.**

Very few wills are successfully challenged; most are upheld by courts. However, when a will is contested, it adds time and cost to the process of distributing the deceased's assets.

A way to avoid probate is to put assets into a trust known as a "living trust." While you are alive, you are the recipient of the income generated from the living trust's assets. After your death, the trust's assets are disbursed directly to your beneficiaries without having to go through probate. While a living trust avoids probate, it does not avoid income or estate taxes.

Another way to pass assets is by establishing a beneficiary designation. Mutual funds, life insurance, and retirement savings plans are usually passed in this manner.

READY TO LIVE, READY TO DIE

A wise man once said, "You are not ready to live until you are ready to die."

A well-designed estate plan often utilizes more than one methodology for getting the right asset to the right person at the right time under the right circumstances. How you structure ownership of your assets and the rights of your survivors is a critical part of your estate planning.

A well-designed estate plan gives you peace of mind, purpose, and a sense that all will be well after you die. The act of designing an estate plan need not be morbid, and it shouldn't make you sad. Designing an estate plan should make you feel liberated, that you can live life to the fullest knowing that should anything happen to you, your loved ones will be able to carry on without financial hardship or frustration.

When first designing an estate plan, you should imagine dying tomorrow. As unpleasant as that may seem, look at your asset inventory and determine whom you would like to have each of your assets. Determine if you wish to leave a public legacy after your death by giving some of your assets to organizations that do the kind of political, civic, educational, religious, or charitable work you feel is important.

As with life and nature itself, all beneficiaries are not created equal. Your estate plan needs to take into account a number of contingencies. Beneficiaries may be different from one another because of disability or permanent health issues. You may feel a need to set aside a greater portion of your estate for a disabled or ill beneficiary, or a lesser portion of your estate for a beneficiary whose lifestyle you disapprove of and feel is inappropriate to support.

In addition, you should plan for the unlikely event that you and your beneficiary die in a common accident. You should have contingencies in your estate for this possibility, such as a common-accident provision in your wills. Although most attorneys routinely put this provision into wills, many insurance agents fail to include this provision in the life insurance policies they sell to their clients. You should check to see if your policies have one. A LEAP practitioner, who is trained to think of your financial life in a holistic fashion, can make sure this provision is in your life insurance, and can work with you to coordinate all the provisions of your estate plan.

You may die in an accident for which you were at fault, leaving your estate—and your beneficiaries—vulnerable to a judgment from a lawsuit. Putting your assets in a living trust shields them from such a suit.

If the assets in your estate are insufficient for your beneficiaries to live the life you wish them to live, you should fill the gap with additional life insurance. Life insurance is the only asset that allows you to build an estate instantly and provide the funds necessary to achieve that goal.

Conservation of Assets

The goal in designing an asset-passing strategy is for assets to pass in a way that is simple, efficient, and avoids unnecessary costs, taxes, and expenses.

The bottom line is that you don't want assets tied up in probate court for any length of time. Attorney's fees and court costs mount quickly, cutting into the estate's value. There is no reason for anyone other than your beneficiaries to receive a large portion of your estate. In many cases, a significant portion of an estate has been lost because inappropriate estate-planning techniques led to excessive costs, fees, and taxes.

If an estate plan is well designed at the outset, there is less reason to continuously rework the plan. The number of trusts should be kept to a minimum, to minimize the expense of keeping the trusts current with estate tax laws. I remember a client telling me that the only person who understood his estate plan was his attorney, who had drawn it up. He said that the estate plan was so complex that he had to keep this attorney because he was the only one who understood the plan. That is just plain silly; if you don't understand your estate plan, how do you know if it does what you want it to do?

THE "LAST EXPERT" SYNDROME

Unfortunately, many people have an estate plan that is a product of the last expert they spoke to about the subject. If the last expert was an accountant, the estate plan is heavy on tax-planning "solutions." If the last expert was an attorney, the estate plan is bulging with legal-document "solutions." If the last expert was a life insurance agent, the estate plan is overflowing with life-insurance "solutions." If the last expert was a banker, the estate plan has a bank trust as its "solution." All of these may lack a holistic view of an integrated and coordinated estate plan that will hold up over time and be successful no matter what the economic, tax, or legal climate.

The best estate plan uses a coordinated approach, utilizing all of these experts and their solutions in the proper proportion. **This is where the "macro manager" concept of the Lifetime Economic Acceleration Process (LEAP) comes into play. Working on your estate plan with a LEAP practitioner allows you to develop a coordinated plan that utilizes expertise of attorneys, accountants, life insurance companies, and banks as integrated pieces of the same plan, with proper balance and coordination.**

The LEAP practitioner assists you in selecting estate-planning techniques to distribute your assets quickly and efficiently, and helps avoid court costs, probate fees, estate expenses, and distribution challenges from unwanted beneficiaries or government agencies. The LEAP practitioner can help you select charitable alternatives as well, so that you can build on a living legacy.

Income Tax and Estate Tax Planning

There are four different taxes that may come into play in estate planning:

> 1. federal estate tax
> 2. federal income tax
> 3. state inheritance tax, and finally
> 4. state income taxes

A properly designed estate plan can help reduce, minimize, or even eliminate your estate liability for all of these taxes.

But be careful—the tax may not be the biggest issue in your estate plan. There may be other more important issues that could override any effective tax planning.

INCOME TAXES

An important, and often neglected, piece of an estate plan is the income-tax liability exit strategy. This is necessary because so many people have a large portion of their wealth in pretax or tax-deferred retirement savings plans.

At the time of your death, your retirement savings plans will distribute the funds to a named beneficiary. If the beneficiary elects to take the money as a lump-sum distribution, he or she incurs income taxes on the proceeds, just as if you had taken the money as a lump-sum distribution if you were alive. The beneficiary can elect to continue deferring the taxes by "rolling over" the proceeds into his or her retirement savings plan. But the beneficiary cannot avoid paying income taxes at some point. Some beneficiaries are shocked when they take the proceeds out of a retirement savings plan, spend the money, and then get hit with a large income tax bill later.

There are ways for you to reduce, eliminate, or at least minimize the income taxes owed on pretax and tax-deferred retirement savings plan holdings that pass to your beneficiaries. These strategies involve creating planned tax deductions, tax credits, or tax offsets to neutralize the income-tax liability to beneficiaries at the time of death. These include, among others:

- mortgage deductions
- depreciation on investment real estate
- income from a reverse mortgage
- tax-shelter credits
- charitable remainder trust income and deductions
- asset pay-down strategies

All or some of these strategies should be available at retirement time by preparing for their inclusion today and every year before retirement. It will be too late if you or your beneficiaries try to set them up at the time of retirement or death. LEAP practitioners have the knowledge and know-how to help design income-tax exit strategies for estate-planning purposes. They can help you see clearly the magnitude of the income-tax problem in your estate; help you realize that designing an exit strategy need not be complex; and help you understand that the longer you wait, the larger the income-tax liability becomes and the more difficult it is to design a successful working strategy.

A LEAP practitioner can help you restructure your financial situation today so your assets are coordinated with one another. Assets that work together are so much more powerful than assets that are singular and work alone. Many people lose millions of dollars without knowing it because they have not had their money or assets coordinated. This provides you with more flexibility, as well as more asset protection and income-tax deductions. This can all be done with little or in most cases no additional out-of-pocket outlays on your part. All it takes is a little know-how and logic. These techniques will work under any set of circumstances, whatever your income or estate size. They guarantee that your wealth will not be entirely or in large part lost to you or your beneficiaries.

ESTATE TAXES

The estate tax was established as a way to redistribute wealth and not allow too much of the nation's wealth to perpetually end up in the hands of a few families, as had happened in much of Europe and at the turn of the twentieth century in America. A handful of families such as the Morgans, Carnegies, and Rockefellers controlled essentially all of the raw land, steel, oil, railroads, and waterways in the productive areas of the country. Today, everyone is in some way impacted by the estate or inheritance taxes, even if not directly. If your estate is large enough, these taxes can wreak havoc on your estate, especially in non-liquid estates.

I have two goals with regard to the estate tax. First, to make sure that, whenever possible, clients stay below the threshold at which an estate generates an estate-tax liability. Second, if a client's estate does go over the threshold that triggers an estate-tax liability, to find simple and low-cost ways for the beneficiaries to minimize the estate-tax burden they face.

There are a host of tools you can use to minimize the estate-tax burden on your beneficiaries, regardless of the tax conditions when you die. These include life insurance, testamentary trusts, marital trusts, various gifting techniques, family limited partnerships, reverse mortgages on your home, charitable remainder trusts, and dynasty trusts.

If you are going to use a trust vehicle of some kind, keep in mind that there are potential pitfalls with trust planning. The language of the trust must be continually reviewed to make sure it conforms with current legal and tax rules. Selection of trustees can also be difficult. Not only do you need to guard against theft and fraud, but you need to make sure the trustee will distribute assets according to your wishes, and not according to how he or she generates the most fees from trust management. What looks good on paper may not have any real advantages in flesh-and-blood live scenarios. The courts are filled to the brim with trust arguments by everyone from the IRS, to unpaid creditors, to unhappy beneficiaries.

What can happen will happen, unless you plan properly to avoid it.

Since estate-tax laws are constantly changing, your plan must be kept flexible. Any solution to the estate-tax issue must not be viewed from one set of current tax laws. Too many times I've seen an attorney set up irrevocable trusts to help reduce the estate tax, and then the tax law changes and the trust becomes inoperative.

A well-designed estate plan foresees change and plans for its eventuality. **The test of a good estate plan is one that will hold up under any set of estate-tax laws.** Unfortunately, there are too many attorneys and other advisors who do not have the same view and focus only on current tax laws. This type of plan is doomed to failure, will need to be constantly updated, and will end up being very expensive to manage.

Legacy Planning

I spend part of my time living in Florida. One day I was driving behind a very large Cadillac being driven by a man smoking a very large cigar. On his back bumper was a sticker that read "I'm spending my children's inheritance."

I can't argue that this isn't a legitimate and viable estate plan. I have heard some estate-planning experts say that your goal should be to spend your last dollar at the moment you take your last breath.

But to me that seems shortsighted. How many of us know our family tree? How many of us know how hard our ancestors worked to get us where we are today? Most people reading this book, I dare say, have parents or grandparents or great-grandparents who came to North America to make a better life for their children. They worked hard, often working two jobs, earned, saved, and put off buying things they wanted. They wanted their children to enjoy a better way of life and promoted the American or Canadian dream.

I, like many people, wish to leave a legacy that goes beyond my own needs and those of my wife, children, and grandchildren. Part of that legacy is in the work I do and the business I have built. But in addition I want to leave part of my estate to charities and other institutions that I consider a valuable part of our society. If we can't give back to our nation and to all of the people who have helped us earn what we have, then we are all in trouble. There are many unfortunate people in the world, and wouldn't it feel good to know that we have contributed to helping them have a better life, as our parents did for us?

Estate planning is perhaps the most personal set of decisions you will make in your lifetime. The truth is that at some time, now or in the future, every dollar you have at the time of your death will be spent. The decisions you make in your estate plan will determine who will get a chance to spend them—your family, government, attorneys, or specific charities and other institutions that perform what you see as a social good. The government might spend your money on things you would not necessarily approve of. But if you are in control of how your money will be spent, you will feel good inside. You are a success.

There are many rewards to legacy planning. Some of them are psychological, knowing that when you die you will make a contribution to the ongoing work of charities and other institutions you value. You know that your money will be used for good.

And you don't have to disinherit your children in order to leave a public legacy; you can provide for them as well. In fact, you may have done better by your children than you would have by giving them everything outright. You may spur your children by your example to also give back to the world, both in their lifetime and later at the time of their own death.

At the end of the day, a well-designed and well-thought-out estate plan can be a win-win-win proposition for everyone. The person driving that big car with no plans but to spend it all may die unexpectedly and the money will be lost—and so will his legacy. No one will ever know that he was once here on Earth.

There are also rewards to legacy planning that come in the form of tax deductions, credits, or offsets that can be used in a very purposeful way to reduce income and estate taxes you or your beneficiaries would otherwise have had to pay. Gifts and tax benefits can be current or deferred. They are a win for you, because you know your family is prepared for your death and the world will be a better place for your having lived. They are a win for your children, because they will inherit not only money, but personal values from you. And they are a win for society, because charities and other institutions you believe to be valuable will be able to carry on their good work.

But to make your estate plan a win-win-win come true, you need to take action now and keep it up-to-date throughout your life. It is a mature and responsible outlook and the sign of a successful person. No one can take your success from you no matter what happens. Your life will feel more complete at your accomplishments, no matter how small or how large your estate.

Life insurance can play a role in your estate planning as well. Life insurance is frequently used to pay the taxes due on any estate so beneficiaries do not need to sell other assets and incur other taxes on those asset sales. Life insurance is also used to provide income so other assets can be given to charity, providing tax deductions that offset taxes owed on money coming out of tax-deferred retirement plans.

In summary, not only is life insurance an important part of your wealth-building and wealth-preservation process during your lifetime, it can also serve a vital purpose in wealth preservation at the time of your death, and in the creation of tax strategies. But in order to use your life insurance in all these ways, it must be approached in a highly skilled and professional manner. You need an expert in these matters to help you coordinate and integrate the uses of insurance, while helping you build wealth and save premium dollars.

KEY POINTS
• Insure your life to full economic value.
• Whole life is the king of all policies, providing the most benefits.
• Term life, universal life, variable life, and survivorship life are specialized life-insurance products that fit particular situations but are not right for everyone.
• Create an estate plan that offers the most flexibility in order to meet changing circumstances, and that provides the most benefits to your family and society.
• Include life insurance in estate-planning decisions because it can provide wealth protection and tax strategies for your beneficiaries.

CHAPTER 9

College Funding

Like most parents, you wish for your children to have the best possible education. No matter what career choices your children make, you want them to have a good start in life. College funding is perhaps the most important family financial decision you will make. Amazingly, many families are making it all wrong.

A number of various tax-advantaged college savings plans have been designed and marketed to the public. Be careful. Many of these plans have the same drawbacks as other tax-advantaged plans if they are designed to simply accumulate funds over time for a particular need.

These tax-advantaged savings plans are simply designated for college costs and therefore have only one use. That means that your money is not working for you and getting a multiplier effect. Tying up your money for the goal of providing your children's college funds, although admirable and well-meaning, leads to many lost opportunities and costs.

The questions you should be asking of your college-funding strategy are: How can I pay for college and get all my money back? And how can I guarantee my children's education even if I become disabled or die, the market declines, interest rates drop, I get sued, or college costs skyrocket?

Most people's plans simply do not provide for such contingencies. They have been taught to establish a goal or target of having only the money they'll need, then decide on how much to put away toward that end. This type of planning may be a serious losing strategy in terms of wealth building and wealth protection. The money you pay the college is lost to you and you will never see it again for other uses.

Even if the college-funding technique you use is income-tax deferred, or even income-tax free, it may not be appropriate. What is the point of having the earnings tax-free and then giving all the money to the college? The ideal method in the Lifetime Economic Acceleration Process (LEAP) is to use your money over and over again and not lose it for any reason. Earmarking funds for college and getting only one use on your money is wasteful and inefficient. Your money is tied up, and you have no control over its use. You are going to lose your money's potential, and eventually the money itself.

Using money for just one purpose has a cost. Putting your money into one account and letting it grow keeps your money out of play. What would happen if you became disabled? Should your children not go to school just because you became disabled? College-specific savings plans won't help you. Contributions to them will simply stop.

What if you die before your children get to college? Will your children not go to school simply because you died? Those college-funding plans won't help you. There are no death benefits attached.

What if the investment assets within the college account go down in value due to market fluctuation? You may not have enough money set aside to pay for your children's education, and you will have to come up with more money. You also are not allowed to write off any losses on your tax return if you lose money in college-funding plans.

All of these disadvantages of pre-designed tax-advantaged college-funding plans are not even the main problem. If you have funds set aside for college in a pre-designed college-funding plan, that money must be spent on college costs. What if your child doesn't go to college? Your tax deferral is gone and you will pay income taxes at your ordinary income tax rates when you take the money out of the plan, rather than paying capital gains taxes.

But even if your child does go to college, once the money has been used to pay for college, you have no more use of it. It is gone. It no longer is available to you to use again and again for other needs, such as retirement. The main problem, then, is that these plans have a large lost-opportunity cost.

Say you have saved $250,000 in a pre-designed tax-qualified college-funding plan. Assume you are 45 years old when these funds have been fully spent for college costs. Once you have spent the $250,000 on college costs, the money is gone forever. That means that in twenty years, at your retirement at age 65, you don't have it to use for retirement income.

If you had not spent the $250,000 for college, you would have had $1,681,000, if you assume that you could have invested the $250,000 at 10 percent a year for twenty years. That's a staggering figure. That money would be worth at least $160,000 in annual retirement income beginning at age 65. That is an expensive college education your children will cost you!

And if you did not touch the money for retirement income at age 65 and let it continue to grow for another twenty years, until you were 85 years old, you would have $11,308,000. (Your children would be better off not going to college and waiting for their inheritance!) All kidding aside, you need to have your cake and eat it too. How do you get your children educated without losing all of that money?

What Should You Do?

How can you pay for college and retain the opportunity to utilize your money again later for retirement income?

You should start college planning early in your children's lives. You should avoid using a pre-designed product for college funding. Do not tie up money and keep it in one place for only one use. Winning that game is difficult. People fail to realize the lost-opportunity cost of these programs because they have been taught to focus on the need for funds rather than on the efficient use of money. They get caught up in the emotional aspect of college education for their children, which is the battle, while they lose the war.

One of the keys to sound planning for college is not to relinquish all of your assets in order to fund your children's college education costs. Instead, an efficient and effective strategy is to simultaneously take advantage of every possible aid program, tax advantage, leveraging technique, and cash-flow strategy available. This allows you to maintain the greatest amount of wealth-building potential possible. The best plan is a combination of financial products and strategies, not one product acting alone.

EDUCATION FUNDING: A LIVING BENEFIT OF WHOLE-LIFE INSURANCE

In the chapter on insurance, I spoke about the "living benefits" of whole-life insurance. There is no better example of how these living benefits can be utilized than in the case of funding a child's college education. Whole-life insurance can make funds available for college whether you live, die, or become disabled. How the whole-life policy provides for college funds in the event of death or disability is rather straightforward, and explained in the chapter on life insurance.

The most interesting use of whole life, however, is as a living vehicle for college funding. Remember, cash value and dividends build up inside a whole-life insurance policy tax-deferred, the same way they do in stand-alone college-funding plans. If you acquired a whole-life policy on the life of each parent when your oldest child turned 5, by the time your child entered college, there would be at least thirteen years of accumulated dividends and cash values in the policies. There would be no income taxes, no disability to worry about, and no premature death that could disrupt the plan. There would be no market fluctuation to take away funds, nothing but steady growth.

Now we are ready for the good part. In the traditional approach to college funding, college costs are spent from the college funds and the cost cannot be recaptured or minimized. As I said earlier, the cost of college funding becomes a lost-opportunity cost with regard to future wealth building.

But if you borrow the cost of college from the insurance company, using the cash values and dividends in the whole-life insurance policies as collateral, you still have a death benefit that would be greater than the borrowed funds should you die. Your cash value is still in the policy. The good news is that you never have to pay back the policy loan, since loans from life insurance do not have to be repaid.

Even though this is a good option, it is actually not the game plan I recommend.

A better way to accomplish the same thing is to use other borrowed funds for college expenses, such as federal college loans, a home mortgage, and a home-equity loan or line of credit. The life-insurance-policy dividends and cash value can be used as collateral on the loan. Such a loan may be fully or partially tax-deductible.

In either of these instances, instead of using your own accumulated funds for college costs, you are using other people's money and using your conserved asset pool and its interest to pay the loans back. By age 65, you could have conserved all of your own money and have a death benefit that can be used for other enhanced retirement-planning strategies.

By using a whole-life insurance policy as your major college-funding device, you obtain the following benefits:

- tax deferral
- disability protection
- premature-death protection
- possible creditor protection
- qualify for financial aid (possibly)
- convert term-life insurance costs (if applicable)
- liquidity without penalty
- no stock-market losses
- no income taxes
- peace of mind
- elimination of lost-opportunity cost
- enhanced retirement income
- estate planning

No other financial instrument can provide all of these benefits at once. There is no question that if you start college planning while your children are under the age of 10, whole-life insurance is a major part of a superior college-funding strategy when coordinated with your other assets.

COLLEGE FUNDING FOR OLDER CHILDREN

If your children are over the age of 10, other products and strategies become more important. These include a mortgage, a home-equity loan or line of credit, 529 college-savings plans, Coverdell Education savings plans, Uniform Gift to Minors Act (UGMA) accounts, U.S. Savings Bonds, or laddered certificates of deposits or government bonds. But whole life still has a role to play. Keep in mind that your goal is to not use your own money. Try to use other people's money as long as your money acts as collateral. Pay back with the earnings on your money, not the principal. Take as many tax deductions for college costs as you can. Use inflationary dollars over time to pay back the loans you took with other people's money.

All in all, college funding comes from a well-orchestrated financial plan and not from any one product. You should be achieving many uses with your money and not tying it up in order to achieve a single need or goal. A LEAP practitioner can help you design a proper course of action that meets your desires to have your children educated while maintaining and protecting your long-term wealth-building capabilities.

> ## KEY POINTS
> • Avoid any one product for your college-funding plans.
> • Avoid giving all of your money to the college and experiencing a lost-opportunity cost.
> • The best strategy is a well-balanced use of a variety of different financial tools.

CHAPTER 10

Retirement Savings

As I have stated throughout this book, there are advantages and disadvantages to every financial product or plan. And so it is with pretax retirement savings plans such as 401(k), TSA, Keogh, Simplified IRA, pension, or profit-sharing plans. Although saving for retirement is a worthwhile and necessary financial pursuit, one must be careful not to overuse any one source of retirement funds and to truly understand the consequences of such action. The "golden years" should be happy and fruitful, a time to enjoy life after all your years of labor. Yet pretax retirement savings plans are still the financial product that is most misunderstood by both financial advisors and the public at large.

People will often give me at least one of six reasons or advantages for investing in pretax retirement savings plans.

Reason #1: **"I save taxes."**
Reason #2: **"I get an employer match."**
Reason #3: **"I pay no taxes on the annual growth in the account."**
Reason #4: **"When I retire, I'll pay my taxes in a lower tax bracket."**
Reason #5: **"It is easy to do: It is payroll deducted."**
Reason #6: **"I will have amassed money for my retirement."**

Let's take a careful look at each one of these advantages or reasons that people give for why they invest in pretax retirement savings plans.

REASON #1: "I save taxes."

As I've already stated throughout this book, income taxes are the biggest wealth-eroding factor for each and every citizen. Since pretax retirement savings plans are promoted by financial institutions as a tax savings device, a fairly large percentage of the population believes that they are saving taxes when they participate in a pretax retirement savings program through their employer or in a personal plan. But as I'll explain more thoroughly in this chapter, you most likely will not save income taxes and may even pay more in taxes over the long term by using such a plan. The misunderstanding lies in the words "tax savings" rather than the more accurate term "tax deferral." Pretax retirement savings plans do not save taxes, they only defer them. There is no income-tax savings in any year that you deposit money into a pretax retirement savings plan, only a deferral of those income taxes until the time you withdraw the money from the plan.

REASON #2: "I get an employer match."

Many employers that sponsor retirement savings plans will partially or fully "match" each employee's contribution to the plan. Not all employers match employee contributions to the plan, but many do. For example, an employer might match fifty cents for every dollar from the employee, up to 3 percent of the employee's total salary. Getting a match from an employer is a good thing and certainly adds to the value of the pretax retirement savings plan. Without an employer match, the disadvantages of a pretax retirement plan are a more serious problem.

Many people think, and many financial advisors counsel, that when an employer provides a 50 percent match, the employee is earning 50 percent on his or her money. I have had people tell me that they could not invest money and get a 50 percent rate of return anywhere, so that makes the pretax qualified plan a no-brainer. To them, the math works something like this: "I put in $1,000. My employer puts in $500. My investment has earned 50 percent immediately. What could be better?"

If you could take the $1,500 and go spend it immediately, it would be true that your $1,000 had, in effect, earned 50 percent immediately. But remember that retirement savings plans cannot be tapped until you are at least retirement age, so there is a time lag between the time you put the money into the plan and the time it can be expended.

The true way to calculate the value of the 50 percent match by the employer is to compare the difference between an annual $1,000 contribution without a 50 percent match and an annual $1,500 contribution (your $1,000 plus your employer's $500), both earning the same rate of return over the same length of time. Let me show you.

Let's say you made an annual $1,000 contribution into a pretax retirement savings account, which earned 8 percent a year. After thirty years, those $1,000 contributions would be worth $122,345. If your employer matched the contribution with $500, at the end of thirty years at 8 percent, the $1,500 annual contributions would be worth $183,518. That is 50 percent percent more than you would have had with just your own $1,000 contributions, which is perfectly logical.

However, that does not equate to a "50 percent rate of return on your money," as many financial advisors and the public think. What you need to do is to determine the rate of return that $1,000 would have to earn in order to have $183,518 in thirty years. This calculation gives you an annual rate of return of 9.47 percent.

In other words, you would have had to earn an annual rate of return of 9.47 percent annually for thirty years on your $1,000 in order to end up with the same amount you ended up with by investing $1,500 that earned 8 percent annually. This means that the $500 employer match equated to an extra rate of return of only 1.47 percent annually over thirty years, and not 50 percent annually.

So, next time you hear someone say that you are receiving a "50 percent return on your money through the company match," you will realize that you are not getting a 50 percent annual rate of return. If you did get a 50 percent rate of return on just a $1,000 annual contribution, it would total $575,250,000 in thirty years. That certainly is not the case. So do not let people hype you into thinking that you are getting a 50 percent rate of return.

Again, when there is an employer match, it is better than without one. It adds to your money the amount that will be accumulated in the account. I usually advise people who have such an employer-matched account to invest their money each year into a secure savings-account-type investment and use the employer match to invest in equities where there is higher risk. This way, your money that you worked hard for is secure for retirement, while you are only taking risks with the employer's money. Many clients like that idea and have found it to be helpful through both good times and bad times in the market.

REASON #3: "I pay no taxes on the annual growth in the account."

By deferring the tax each year, you are keeping more of your money rather than paying tax each and every year. People feel good knowing that the growth of their account is compounding without a current tax, which increases the growth of the account even more. But this approach may or may not be to your advantage, as I'll explain later in this chapter. The tax rules change and are set up in such a way that any deferral of tax can have negative consequences for many people. If you amass enough money for retirement, which you should, then there is a good chance that the amount of tax deferral will be significant, and this can put you into the highest income- and estate-tax brackets.

REASON #4: "When I retire, I'll pay my taxes in a lower tax bracket."

This is the jackpot, the pot of gold at the end of the rainbow. Everybody believes that when they retire, they will be in a lower tax bracket than when they were making contributions to the plan. But for many retirees, especially low- and middle-income people who have accumulated significant tax-deferred retirement savings, this may not be true. For many individuals, they will actually be in a higher tax bracket, for one of three reasons:

- **The accumulation of money in the account can produce a large retirement income, and when added to other income sources, that raises their tax bracket.**
- **The tax law can change and it's possible that their tax rate will be higher when they retire.**
- **They may end up in a higher tax bracket anyway, often because they no longer have deductions such as home mortgage interest or dependents such as minor children.**

Why would anyone want their retirement income to be so low as to be in a low tax bracket? That contradicts the purpose of retirement planning. Your income should be as high as when you were working in order to maintain the same lifestyle. Everyone should have the goal of being in the same or even a higher tax bracket at retirement age. That would be financial success. But most people are preparing for financial failure by being told that they will be in a lower tax bracket. They are setting themselves up for disappointment. Why would a 64-year-old person want to have a work income that produces one standard of living, and then only one year later retire, effectively taking a "pay cut," and have a lower standard of living?

Could it be that the financial institutions want to make pretax retirement plans appear to be a tax benefit by promoting moving people to a lower tax bracket, but at the same time they are promoting financial planning to accumulate wealth so that you can be in a higher tax bracket and enjoy your retirement? Be careful when reading or listening to so-called advisors claiming that you will be in a lower tax bracket. If that will be the case, then that advisor has failed you in your overall retirement planning.

REASON #5: "It is easy to do: It is payroll deducted."

One of the nice things about pretax retirement savings plans is that they are payroll deducted. This acts as a forced savings and is very convenient. But now you are limited to the investment choices of your employer. Some have a wide range of choices, while others have a limited range. Some employers only allow you to invest in their own company stock. No matter how many choices you have, you still are not allowed to invest pretax qualified plan money in many areas that personal funds could invest in, such as real estate. You may not have an advisor to help you manage the money in your pretax retirement savings plan. The task of management is up to you, and most people do not have the time or the knowledge to manage the money successfully.

REASON #6: "I will have amassed money for my retirement."

This is the best reason to have money in a pretax retirement savings plan. All of the other reasons are debatable and uncertain as to their benefits. You need money when you are retired. Pretax retirement plans are one good vehicle for saving for that purpose. However, they should not get all of your retirement dollars. There must be balance in your retirement planning assets in order for your retirement to be secure and safe. You will need other liquid dollars in case the age of distribution is moved to age 70. You will need other tax deductions to offset the income from the retirement account. You will need life insurance to protect the assets from estate and income taxes if you die with the money in the plan. You will need other guaranteed sources of income to protect against interest-rate or market declines.

Putting all of your eggs in one basket is never a good idea, and that rule applies to pretax retirement savings plans as well. Millions of people have lost money in their pretax retirement savings plans over the last several years and have had nothing else to fall back on, other than Social Security, which in most cases is too little to retire on.

A Tax Break Today, a Tax Break Tomorrow, but Ultimately a Tax Bill

The biggest perceived benefit of all retirement savings plans is their tax benefit. Some plans you fund with pretax dollars, while others you fund with post-tax dollars. What is the difference?

A pretax plan is one in which your money goes into the plan directly from your earned income. You are not taxed on the money that goes into the plan and the money accumulates tax-deferred. You only pay taxes when you take the money out of the plan.

A post-tax plan is one where you contribute money to the plan after you have paid tax on it, but the accumulation of money within the plan is tax-deferred. You only pay taxes on the growth of the plan when you take out your money.

A few plans are funded with after-tax dollars and offer truly tax-free accumulation (e.g., Roth IRAs in the United States). These plans are better than simply having a tax-deferred plan.

Pretax Retirement Plans

There are many misunderstandings about pretax retirement plans. It is true that the money you contribute from your earned income does not appear on your income tax statement for the year it was contributed. However, tax on this income is only deferred; that means that the income tax on this money is postponed until it is taken out of the plan later. You still have a tax obligation on the money, but you are postponing it. You are not "saving" taxes, only putting them off. It is wrong to say that taxes had been saved. You will read, hear, and be given much misinformation that you have saved taxes by putting money into a pretax retirement savings plan. This is simply not true.

The tax benefit from any contribution you make to a pretax retirement savings plan is locked up in the plan; it is also not free for you to spend, as many financial advisors and pundits make it out to be. For example, let's say you earn $75,000 and contribute $5,000 to a pretax retirement savings plan. Your coworker in the next workspace earns the same amount of income as you do, but she does not put any money into the pretax retirement savings plan. **Figure 10.1** shows the difference in your tax obligations.

Figure 10.1

YOU		COWORKER
$75,000	Earned income	$75,000
$ 5,000	RSP contribution	$0
$70,000	Taxable income	$75,000
$14,000	Taxes paid	$15,500

You have a lower taxable income than your coworker because of your contribution to the retirement savings plan; you pay $14,000 in income taxes while your coworker pays $15,500 in income taxes for the year. But just because you paid $1,500 less in taxes does not mean that you have saved $1,500 in income taxes and have that money in your pocket, for you do not. Let's see why in **Figure 10.2.**

Figure 10.2

YOU		COWORKER
$75,000	Earned income	$75,000
$ 5,000	RSP contribution	$0
$70,000	Taxable income	$75,000
$14,000	Taxes paid	$15,500
$56,000	Dollars for spending	$59,500

The dollars for spending are simply derived by subtracting the tax paid from the taxable income. Now let's assume that you and your co-worker have identical necessary living expenses, $56,000. Do either of you have anything left over? Look at **Figure 10.3.**

Figure 10.3

YOU		COWORKER
$56,000	Dollars for spending	$59,500
$56,000	Living expenses	$56,000
$0	Cash to invest	$ 3,500

After paying your annual and necessary living expenses, you have no money left over to invest, while your coworker has $3,500 left.

"Okay," you say. "But I have already invested, in my retirement savings plan. And I was able to invest $5,000 while my friend can only invest $3,500." True enough. So you have an extra $1,500. But where is it? It is in your retirement account. It is not in your pocket. If your coworker takes her $3,500 and invests it into the same investment that you have in your retirement account, the only difference between the two of you is that you have $1,500 more invested. But you both now have nothing left over to invest.

DON'T COUNT THE TAX SAVING TWICE

So the big question is, how do you have a tax savings in your pocket? You do not—it is in the plan. You can't count it twice. What many financial advisors and news media state is that there is a tax savings in your pocket too. They want you to believe that you have an extra $1,500 in your pocket. All of the benefits that they claim about pretax retirement savings plans are overstated and misleading. Do not be fooled by such claims. The tax savings is only in the plan and not in your pocket.

In my seminars, I emphasize the fallacy of claims that there is a tax savings in pretax retirement plans by using this analogy. If it were true that because your income was reduced by the RSP, that you saved taxes, and can now invest them, then the best tax shelter would be to quit your job. Then you would not have any taxes to pay, and you could take the tax savings and sit back and invest them for the rest of your life. How easy life would be by not working and saving those taxes and investing them each and every year. Sounds silly, but that is what the financial advisors are claiming by telling you that there is another tax savings in your pocket in addition to the tax-deferred dollars in the plan.

It should seem patently obvious that this is not the case. Yet so many financial advisors and financial pundits insist that the person who made the contribution to his or her retirement savings account now has the tax savings to use again. Think of it another way. If you were allowed to put your entire $75,000 earned into a retirement savings account, you would have no money to pay your bills. Yes, you would pay $15,500 less in income tax than if you put nothing in the plan. But you wouldn't have that $15,500 to invest.

This double counting of taxes saved is a major error in the thinking of many financial advisors. They continue to provide misinformation to consumers. Remember, money is not math and math is not money. If you put money into a retirement savings account, the tax savings is in the plan, and it can't magically appear in your pocket as well.

AFTER-TAX RETIREMENT SAVINGS PLANS

After-tax retirement savings plans are those plans that only defer taxes on the earnings inside the account, but you pay taxes on the money going into the account. The money that gets contributed to the account has already been taxed as income. Since there is only one tax benefit (tax deferral on the account's earnings) instead of two benefits (tax deferral on both the contribution and the account's earnings), most of these accounts are less advantageous than pretax accounts. Yet they have their advantages too. The advantage of a post-tax retirement savings plan is that there may be no limitation on the amount of money you can contribute as compared to the limitations on pretax plans. (The Roth IRA is the exception to this rule, since you contribute with after-tax dollars, but pay no taxes on the accumulated earnings when you remove the money from your account at retirement.)

The Disadvantages of All Retirement Savings Plans

Are the benefits, laws, programs, and practices regarding retirement plans in consumers' best interests? Not necessarily. The decision to contribute to a retirement savings plan is an individual one, and no general rules should apply. Some people will be far better off never investing in an RSP, depending on their own individual financial circumstances. Others will benefit greatly by investing in an RSP. But for most people, the decision will be a difficult one. There are many factors to consider before such a contribution is made.

Let me give you the disadvantages of retirement savings plans before we can draw some rules to consider.

PROBLEM #1: Penalties for Early Withdrawal

For many families, there are times in life when they must dip into savings to maintain their lifestyle or meet their basic living expenses. These include the loss of a job; an illness to a family member that is not covered or not completely covered by health insurance; the need to relocate; or a major home repair that must be made such as a new roof, a foundation repair, or a rebuilt septic system. (Many of my neighbors in Florida encountered just such circumstances in 2004 due to major hurricane damage not covered by their insurance policies, or high deductibles they could not cover without dipping into their savings.)

If all of a family's savings is locked up inside a retirement savings plan, this necessitates taking money from the retirement pool either by loan or by withdrawal. This may trigger both a tax and an early-withdrawal penalty that would take away any tax benefit one had obtained. Actually, this would result in more taxes having been paid than if the money had been invested outside of the retirement savings plan.

PROBLEM #2: Limited Investment Choices

Many employer-provided tax-deferred retirement savings plans have limited choices as to how employees can invest their money. Most retirement plans do not allow investments in rental property, vacation homes, racehorses, collectibles, or businesses. Most plans only allow contributions to be made into savings accounts, insurance products, or investment companies such as mutual funds. Although some plans provide a fairly wide range of investment companies, these choices are still limited. That presents some dangers for the consumer, since diversification is limited to paper assets. You may have heard or read the many horror stories of individuals whose stock portfolios or mutual funds declined substantially just a year or two before their retirement.

For people who have most of their money in retirement savings plans, it is extremely dangerous to rely so heavily upon the stock market for lifelong financial well-being. There should be more flexibility in investment choices for this type of planning.

For instance, one of the most successfully managed portfolios in the world is that of the Harvard University endowment. It has much of its money in diversified investments including real estate, non-public businesses, and alternative investments.

One should seek to diversify investments not just by asset allocation models in stocks and funds, but also by the type of investments.

PROBLEM #3: No Continuation for Disability or Death

If a person becomes disabled, most contributions to the retirement savings account stop. The family may have to dip into the retirement account to meet living expenses. Even if the family has other resources, the retirement plan will not continue to be funded and will fall far short of retirement income needs. People who have become disabled have suffered in two ways. First, there is the physical and emotional distress of being disabled, and then there is the financial shock that they have no continuation of funding for their retirement. Yet the person is still alive and not able to look forward to a successful financial life because the retirement plan failed him/her at the time of need. This lack of continuation for disability is one of the most devastating financial disadvantages of retirement plans.

In the case of death, a retirement savings plan becomes part of the estate and can be taxed heavily. In addition, as with disability, there is no retirement plan continuation for the survivors if the employee were to die. Whatever money was in the plan at the time of death is all the family will receive, after taxes of course. For young families, this may be a devastating blow to their financial well-being.

PROBLEM #4: Tax Uncertainty

There is no way for you—or anyone—to know what the tax rates and regulations will be when it comes time for you to retire. If the next iteration of taxes seeks to close the current annual deficits and reduce the national debt, rates could go up dramatically in the future.

Money that you deferred taxes on could cost you more in taxes when you withdraw it, even if your income including that withdrawal is lower than your current working income. This has occurred several times in our tax history. This notion about being in a lower tax bracket when one retires may be unrealistic.

In the past, the government levied a surtax on all retirement plans. Not only did people pay the income taxes upon withdrawal, but they had to pay this surtax too. There was a threshold before these surtaxes kicked in, but we can never know what the government's new tax laws will be regarding retirement savings plans. After all, that is where all the money is and they know it.

PROBLEM #5: The Nest Egg That Crushes the Nest

If you are making maximum contributions to your pretax retirement savings account and you are diligent about it, there is no doubt that you might be able to build up a large tax-deferred nest egg. But remember, that nest egg is not yours completely. You have financial institutions, government, and corporations as partners. Financial institutions want their commissions, fees, and charges; government wants taxes; and corporations want your money in the form of inflation and new products.

Figure 10.4 illustrates the situation for an individual who put away $6,000 a year for thirty years into a pretax retirement savings account and has earned an average annual rate of return of 8 percent on the investments. At the end of thirty years, the illustration shows how much money will be in the account.

Figure 10.4

YEAR	ANNUAL PAYMENT	ACCT. BALANCE BEG. OF YEAR	ANNUAL INTEREST	ACCT. BALANCE END OF YEAR
1	(6,000.00)		480.00	6,480
2	(6,000.00)	6,480	998.40	13,478
3	(6,000.00)	13,478	1,558.27	21,037
4	(6,000.00)	21,037	2,162.93	29,200
5	(6,000.00)	29,200	2,815.97	38,016
6	(6,000.00)	38.016	3,521.25	47,537
7	(6,000.00)	47,537	4,282.95	57,820
8	(6,000.00)	57,820	5,105.58	68,925
9	(6,000.00)	68,925	5,994.03	80,919
10	(6,000.00)	80,919	6,953.55	93,873
11	(6,000.00)	93,873	7,989.83	107,863
12	(6,000.00)	107,863	9,109.02	122,972
13	(6,000.00)	122,972	10,317.74	139,290
14	(6,000.00)	139,290	11,623.16	156,913
15	(6,000.00)	156,913	13,033.01	175,946
16	(6,000.00)	175,946	14,555.66	196,501
17	(6,000.00)	196,501	16,200.11	218,701
18	(6,000.00)	218,701	17,976.12	242,678
19	(6,000.00)	242,678	19,894.21	268,572
20	(6,000.00)	268,572	21,965.74	296,538
21	(6,000.00)	296,538	24,203.00	326,741
22	(6,000.00)	326,741	26,619.24	359,360
23	(6,000.00)	359,360	29,228.78	394,589
24	(6,000.00)	394,589	32,047.08	432,636
25	(6,000.00)	432,636	35,090.85	473,726
26	(6,000.00)	473,726	38,378.12	518,105
27	(6,000.00)	518,105	41,928.37	566,033
28	(6,000.00)	566,033	45,762.64	617,796
29	(6,000.00)	617,796	49,903.65	673,699
30	(6,000.00)	673,699	54,375.94	734,075

As you can see from the chart, the RSP will have $734,075 in it after thirty years. **Figure 10.5** shows the effects of a 30 percent tax rate when it comes time to distribute the account. If the person were to take it all out at once—and we will discuss later the merits of taking it all out or taking it in installments—and the tax rate was only 30 percent, it would leave $513,852.

Now, because it is thirty years away, and given a 3 percent annual inflation rate, that money would only buy what $211,700 would buy today. That is a 72 percent wealth erosion.

Figure 10.5

734,075	PAYMENT
(220,223)	Federal Tax 30.00%
513,853	NET INCOME
(302,152)	Inflation @ 3.00% annually
211,700	TODAY'S DOLLARS AT AGE 65

PROBLEM #6: Ordinary Taxes Versus Capital Gains Taxes

Retirement plan rules say you must invest your money in financial assets. Since these accounts are long-term for retirement, one would think that the earnings on the account would receive the tax advantage of long-term capital gains tax rate on the invested capital. But this is not so. All pretax and deferred-tax retirement savings plans will be taxed at the ordinary income tax rates an individual will be subject to at the time the account is disbursed. The capital gains rate may be much lower at the time of disbursement, but consumers forfeit that tax benefit when they join a pretax or post-tax retirement savings plan.

Figure 10.6 shows the difference between identical individuals, one investing in a pretax retirement savings plan and the other not. Person A puts $10,000 into a stock for his retirement account. Person B can only put $7,500 into the stock since he had to pay current income taxes on his $10,000. They both invest the money in the same stock for ten years and receive a 10 percent annual average growth rate on the stock.

Figure 10.6

PRETAX RSP INVESTOR		POST-TAX INVESTOR
$10,000	Amount invested	$7,500
$175,311	Value in 10 years	$131,483
$52,593	Tax paid	$8,472
$122,718	Net after-tax value	$123,011

At the end of ten years, they both liquidate their investment and pay their tax. The pretax RSP investor who paid ordinary income tax rates (30 percent) would have $122,718 at the end of ten years. The post-tax investor, even though he paid tax annually and could only invest $7,500, paid capital-gains tax rates (15 percent) and would have $123,011. The person not investing in a retirement plan came out slightly better. Keep in mind that there are a host of other advantages too. He could put the money in a broader range of investments, not have penalties for early withdrawal, would not be subject to age-of-distribution regulations, and could use the investment as collateral for a loan.

PROBLEM #7: No Tax Write-Offs for Market Losses

In the event that your retirement savings plan experiences market losses in any one year or over a longer period, you can't write off those losses like you can with an investment outside a retirement savings plan.

When you have other investments, you have options. You can offset another investment's gain with the loss you incurred, or you can simply deduct the loss on your income-tax return. Giving up these tax advantages is another consideration you must make before investing all of your money in a retirement savings plan.

PROBLEM #8: Borrowing From a Retirement Savings Plan

One of the worst ways to borrow money is from a retirement savings plan. It should be avoided. Proponents of retirement savings plans tout the ability to borrow from the plan as one of its advantages, but it is not.

First, you can only borrow a limited amount. Second, you must pay back the account over a short period of time. Third, the money you use to pay back the loan has already been taxed; therefore, when you withdraw it from the plan at retirement, it will be taxed for a second time. That is double taxation, and that should be avoided at all costs. Fourth, you receive no income-tax deduction for the interest you pay on the account, yet you will pay tax on the interest you pay on the account when you take it out of the account.

Last, but certainly not least, is the lost-opportunity cost of taking the money out of the plan. The reason you put money in the plan was for it to grow for retirement. So when it is out of the plan, you lose the opportunity for the growth of the money at the end. The cost could be significant.

PROBLEM #9: Loss of Control

Many people do not understand that the money in a retirement savings plan is not your money, yet. You have little if any control over what will happen to it. There are all kinds of government rules and regulations concerning it. You are subject to any future changes government makes in the form of new regulations, and you must accept and abide by them.

For instance, let's say income-tax rates rise to 70 percent again, as they once were for many years. The money you have in your retirement account will get hit with this new tax rate because you have no control or say in the matter. If you have other assets, and the same tax-rate increase occurs, you have choices as to what to do with your money. You may move your money to a tax-free account, or real estate, or capital-gains-generating assets. You have no such options or control with retirement savings plans. You are locked in and vulnerable.

The Importance of Knowing the Disadvantages

As you can see, retirement savings plans have many disadvantages. My purpose is not to tell you not to use them. **My intention is to inform you of the downside of these programs, so that you do not get caught unaware. You deserve to know each and every one of the plan's disadvantages as well as the advantages. Why aren't the media warning the public about these aspects of such plans?**

Retirement plans can play an important role in your financial life. You should have some money in tax-advantaged retirement savings plans. This may sound contradictory to you after my explanation of the disadvantages of qualified plans, but it is not. **I believe that everyone should have a qualified plan, but not in the way they are owned today. There needs to be a better balance between retirement plan assets and other financial vehicles. And you need to have a financial strategy to help avoid or minimize the disadvantages of these plans.**

Because most people with qualified retirement plans have no exit strategy in place, they will get hit with a large tax bill and have their money significantly eroded by inflation. Also, where beneficiaries face both income and estate taxes, survivors may experience tax shock, as most of the assets of the plan will be confiscated by the government.

There are a number of potential solutions. In many ways, understanding the problem is more important than finding "the" solution. Once you understand the difference between trying to amass more money for retirement and having a successful plan that will work under all scenarios, you can begin to appreciate the level of thought, discussion, and strategic-options analysis that goes into real retirement planning. A practitioner of the Lifetime Economic Acceleration Process (LEAP) is available to work with you to do that kind of analysis.

KEY POINTS

- **Pretax retirement plans do not save income taxes, they only defer them.**
- **There are many disadvantages, as well as advantages, of retirement savings plans.**
- **You need a well-balanced approach to retirement that tax-advantaged retirement savings plans cannot provide by themselves.**
- **It is important to have an exit strategy in place today rather than wait and have no options at retirement.**

CHAPTER 11

Real Estate and Mortgages

No matter what your annual income or total wealth, your home is your castle. The first investment that anyone should make is real estate. For most people, that investment should be in a personal residence. Whether your home is a single-family dwelling, condominium, co-op, townhouse, or other type, your home may represent your largest investment of capital.

Considering real estate taxes, homeowner's insurance, maintenance, improvements, heat, gas, electric, water, sewer, garbage collection, and more, your home will represent a cost of millions upon millions of dollars over your lifetime.

Added to all of these costs is the mortgage cost to finance the home purchase. As with all other savings and investments, choosing a home mortgage is difficult because of the misinformation distributed by the media and the financial community, in addition to the many choices available.

The most expensive way to acquire a home is to pay for it with cash. If you have the good fortune to have enough cash to be able to buy a home without a mortgage, you would be using the most expensive approach. Generally, having a mortgage and paying for it over the longest period of time possible will be most advantageous. Although this is contrary to what the public is trained to believe, the evidence is clear and overwhelming to support it. There are three reasons why this is true:

1. You receive a tax deduction for the interest you pay on the loan.
2. If you have a fixed-rate mortgage, over time you pay the mortgage back with dollars that are not only tax-deductible but dollars that are cheaper because of inflation.
3. You do not suffer as large a lost-opportunity cost as a person who buys the house using all cash does. You have your other money available to work for you, and are sometimes able to receive a higher rate of return on that money than the rate you pay for your mortgage interest.

Let me explain how it works.

Suppose three couples, all age 35, want to purchase the same model home in a new housing development. The three homes have a list price of $300,000.

The first couple buy their home with cash, without a mortgage.

The second couple put down $100,000 in cash and take out a fifteen-year mortgage for $200,000, with an interest rate of 5 percent.

The third couple put down $100,000 in cash and take out a thirty-year mortgage for $200,000, also with an interest rate of 5 percent.

Which of these couples made the best financial decision? Given all constant variables, the third couple made the best decision. To arrive at this conclusion, you have to scratch beneath the surface, so please be patient.

Let's look at some numbers to get an understanding of the cost of each home. **Figure 11.1** is a chart that banks and mortgage companies use to argue that consumers would be better off taking out fifteen-year mortgages on their homes.

As **Figure 11.1** shows, couple #1 have no interest cost, while couple #2 pay $84,686 in interest costs over the fifteen-year life of their mortgage. Couple #3 pay even more in interest: $186,512 over thirty years.

It looks from this chart that, over a thirty-year period, couple #1 pay the least for their home, couple #2 the next least, and couple #3 the most. But this only takes into account the actual payments made for the home, either in a cash sale or through a mortgage. It does not account for taxes saved or lost-opportunity costs.

A number of banks and mortgage companies use the numbers in **Figure 11.1** to make the argument that a fifteen-year mortgage is better

Figure 11.1

MONTHS IN ILLUSTRATION: 360	
CASH	0 CUMULATIVE INTEREST COST
AMOUNT: 300,000	
PAYMENT PLAN 1	
DOWN PAYMENT: 100,000 AMOUNT FINANCED: 200,000 MONTHS 180 EST. RATE: 5.00% MONTHLY PAYMENT: (1,581.59)	(84,686) CUMULATIVE INTEREST COST
PAYMENT PLAN 2	
DOWN PAYMENT: 100,000 AMOUNT FINANCED: 200,000 MONTHS: 360 EST. RATE: 5.00% MONTHLY PAYMENT: (1,073.64)	(186,512) CUMULATIVE INTEREST COST

for homeowners than a thirty-year mortgage. These ads usually show two identical homes, with a headline that states: "The home on the right cost more than the home on the left." Of course, the reason they give for the statement is that the homeowner on the right took a thirty-year mortgage while the homeowner on the left used a fifteen-year mortgage. They conclude that because the couple with the fifteen-year mortgage paid less in interest on their mortgage, they "paid less" for the house. This is, in fact, not true.

When I first saw these types of advertisements, I called the insurance and banking commission in the state where I live to complain that the ads were misleading. The commission staff person I spoke with told me that the commission knew the ads were misleading but could not do anything about it since the ads did not state that the overall cost of the home with the thirty-year mortgage was higher, but that the loan interest was higher.

What is so misleading in these ads, which cause so many consumers to incorrectly choose a fifteen-year mortgage over a thirty-year mortgage? There are two basic facts missing from the ads: tax deductions for the interest paid and the lost-opportunity cost for the money paid in.

Figure 11.2

MONTHS IN ILLUSTRATION: 360	C.O.M. 5%
COUPLE #1: CASH AMOUNT: 300,000	(1,340,323) COMPOUND PRINCIPAL & INTEREST COST
COUPLE #2: 15-YEAR MORTGAGE DOWN PAYMENT: 100,000 AMOUNT FINANCED: 200,000 MONTHS 180 EST. RATE: 5.00% MONTHLY PAYMENT: (1,581.59)	(1,340,323) COMPOUND PRINCIPAL & INTEREST COST
COUPLE #3: 30-YEAR MORTGAGE DOWN PAYMENT: 100,000 AMOUNT FINANCED: 200,000 MONTHS: 360 EST. RATE: 5.00% MONTHLY PAYMENT: (1,073.64)	(1,340,323) COMPOUND PRINCIPAL & INTEREST COST

In the rest of this chapter, I'm going to dig a little deeper and show you how and why it may make sense for just about any homeowner to have a thirty-year mortgage and not a fifteen-year mortgage.

Figure 11.2 shows the same variables as **Figure 11.1,** but adds one more item. It is in the skinny box at the top of the chart with the initials C.O.M., which stands for cost of money. The cost of money is the rate of return one could get through an alternative investment—in other words, the lost-opportunity cost for buying the house. For **Figure 11.2,** I've assigned a cost of money as 5 percent.

Look at the three boxes on the right-hand side of the chart. As you can see, if the cost of money is the same as the cost of the mortgage interest for a fifteen-year or thirty-year mortgage, all three couples will "pay" the same amount of money over thirty years—$1,340,323—to buy their houses. They will simply pay the money in different ways.

Couple #1 will pay $300,000 in cash and pay $1,040,323 in lost-opportunity costs on that money over the next thirty years. Couple #2 will pay $100,000 in a down payment, $1,581.59 per month for 180 months, and the rest in lost-opportunity costs. Couple #3 will pay $100,000 in a down payment, $1,073.64 per month for 360 months, and the rest in

Figure 11.3

MONTHS IN ILLUSTRATION: 360 C.O.M. 5% TAX BRACKET: 32%	
COUPLE #1: CASH	(1,340,323) COMPOUND PRINCIPAL & INTEREST COST
AMOUNT: 300,000	
COUPLE #2: 15-YEAR MORTGAGE	(1,340,323) COMPOUND PRINCIPAL & INTEREST COST
DOWN PAYMENT: 100,000	
AMOUNT FINANCED: 200,000	94,177 COMPOUND TAX SAVINGS
MONTHS 180	
EST. RATE: 5.00%	(1,246,146) NET COMPOUND MORTGAGE COST
MONTHLY PAYMENT: (1,581.59)	
COUPLE #3: 30-YEAR MORTGAGE	(1,340,323) COMPOUND PRINCIPAL & INTEREST COST
DOWN PAYMENT: 100,000	
AMOUNT FINANCED: 200,000	162,765 COMPOUND TAX SAVINGS
MONTHS: 360	
EST. RATE: 5.00%	(1,177,558) NET COMPOUND MORTGAGE COST
MONTHLY PAYMENT: (1,073.64)	

lost-opportunity costs.

Now let's start to change some of the variables and see which method of buying a house—cash, a fifteen-year mortgage, or a thirty-year mortgage—is most advantageous.

First, let's look at taxes. This is seen in **Figure 11.3.** To make it fair, we'll say that all three couples are in the same tax bracket, 32 percent. (You can find this by going to the skinny box at the top of the chart again, next to the C.O.M., where it says tax bracket.)

As you can see by looking over at the right-hand boxes, couple #1 have no cumulative tax savings, because they paid cash. Couple #2 have a cumulative tax savings of $94,177, based on the interest they paid during the fifteen years they paid a mortgage. Couple #3 have a cumulative tax savings of $162,765, based on the interest they paid during the thirty years they paid a mortgage. Already, by looking at the line in each box marked "Net Compound Mortgage Cost," you can see that over thirty years, because of the larger tax savings, the thirty-year mortgage is advantageous. Just because of tax savings, couple #3 pay about $70,000 less over thirty years than couple #2, and about $160,000 less than couple #1.

Now let's change one more variable. In **Figure 11.4** I've assigned the

Figure 11.4

MONTHS IN ILLUSTRATION: 360 C.O.M. 7% TAX BRACKET: 32%	
COUPLE #1: CASH AMOUNT: 300,000	(2,434,949) NET COMPOUND MORTGAGE COST COST TO LIVE IN HOME FOR 360 MONTHS (2,134,949)
COUPLE #2: 15-YEAR MORTGAGE DOWN PAYMENT: 100,000 AMOUNT FINANCED: 200,000 MONTHS 180 EST. RATE: 5.00% MONTHLY PAYMENT: (1,581.59)	(2,239,837) COMPOUND PRINCIPAL & INTEREST COST 156,090 COMPOUND TAX SAVINGS (2,083,747) NET COMPOUND MORTGAGE COST COST TO LIVE IN HOME FOR 360 MONTHS (1,783,747)
COUPLE #3: 30-YEAR MORTGAGE DOWN PAYMENT: 100,000 AMOUNT FINANCED: 200,000 MONTHS: 360 EST. RATE: 5.00% MONTHLY PAYMENT: (1,073.64)	(2,121,463) COMPOUND PRINCIPAL & INTEREST COST 250,789 COMPOUND TAX SAVINGS (1,870,675) NET COMPOUND MORTGAGE COST COST TO LIVE IN HOME FOR 360 MONTHS (1,570,675)

cost of money (the lost-opportunity cost) as 7.00 percent, higher than the mortgage rate. Can you guess what will happen?

First of all, everyone's total cost over thirty years for buying their houses goes up. This is because they all incurred more lost-opportunity costs because they invested in their houses instead of alternative investments that could have earned 7 percent per year.

The compound principal and interest line is now different for the three couples because each incur a different amount of lost-opportunity cost, and that lost-opportunity cost costs them more than any mortgage payments they are making. Couple #1 incur the most lost-opportunity cost because they put the most cash into the house purchase. Couple #2 incur more lost-opportunity cost than couple #3 because they are making a larger monthly mortgage payment, and therefore have less money to invest in the 7 percent alternative investment.

Figure 11.5

MONTHS IN ILLUSTRATION: 360 C.O.M. 7% TAX BRACKET: 32%	
COUPLE #1: CASH AMOUNT: 300,000	(2,434,949) NET COMPOUND MORTGAGE COST COST TO LIVE IN HOME FOR 360 MONTHS (2,134,949)
COUPLE #2: 15-YEAR MORTGAGE DOWN PAYMENT: 100,000 AMOUNT FINANCED: 200,000 MONTHS 180 EST. RATE: 4.00% MONTHLY PAYMENT: (1,479.38)	(2,147,539) COMPOUND PRINCIPAL & INTEREST COST 122,628 COMPOUND TAX SAVINGS (2,024,911) NET COMPOUND MORTGAGE COST COST TO LIVE IN HOME FOR 360 MONTHS (1,724,911)
COUPLE #3: 30-YEAR MORTGAGE DOWN PAYMENT: 100,000 AMOUNT FINANCED: 200,000 MONTHS: 360 EST. RATE: 5.00% MONTHLY PAYMENT: (1,073.64)	(2,121,463) COMPOUND PRINCIPAL & INTEREST COST 250,789 COMPOUND TAX SAVINGS (1,870,675) NET COMPOUND MORTGAGE COST COST TO LIVE IN HOME FOR 360 MONTHS (1,570,675)

When you add the larger tax savings from the larger mortgage payments to the difference in lost-opportunity cost, couple #3 end up paying about $213,000 less over thirty years than couple #2 and about $574,000 less over thirty years than couple #1.

Now, many of you have probably been reading this and thinking that I made an error by keeping the mortgage interest rates the same for the fifteen-year and thirty-year mortgages. It is true that a fifteen-year mortgage carries a lower interest rate than a thirty-year mortgage. Do you know why?

That's right: The bank is benefiting by getting the money sooner so it can loan out the money again. The bank is enjoying not having a lost-opportunity cost. So the bank is willing to give you a cheaper rate that costs you more in monthly charges so that you have the lost-opportunity cost instead.

So let's change that for **Figure 11.5.** Let's make the interest rate for the fifteen-year mortgage 4.00 percent and keep the interest rate for the thirty-year mortgage at 5.00 percent.

To be sure, the gap between the total cost over thirty years of the fifteen-year mortgage as opposed to the thirty-year mortgage is reduced, from about $213,000 to about $154,000. This means that a "spread" of 1 percent between the fifteen-year and thirty-year interest rates does not provide an advantage to the fifteen-year mortgagee. The spread between the fifteen-year and thirty-year mortgage rates would have to be somewhere between 3.5 and 3.75 percent before the true cost over thirty years of a fifteen-year mortgage would be as low as the true cost of a thirty-year mortgage.

So what is the bottom line? It is this:

> - **If you are in the 7 percent tax bracket or above, and**
> - **if there are alternative investments that can earn at least 2 percent more than the interest rate on a thirty-year mortgage, and**
> - **unless the interest rate on a fifteen-year mortgage is 1.75 percent below the rate on a thirty-year mortgage, and**
> - **if you plan to hold the mortgage for at least fifteen years,**
> - **you should take out a thirty-year mortgage as compared to a fifteen-year mortgage.**

Some people ignore the economics and the expenses and cost. They simply want to own their home in fifteen years and do not want to structure any financial plan to improve their situation. It is more of a peace-of-mind transaction for them. They will choose a fifteen-year mortgage.

Investment Properties

If you have the desire to invest in real estate, rental properties can be a winning strategy. This book is not about buying real estate; there are plenty of books on the market if you are interested in that subject. But my purpose here is to say that as an investment, real estate has been an attractive alternative for many investors. Not that it does not have any risk, for it most certainly does. But that risk can be minimized or even offset by the advantages that are contained in investment real estate.

Real estate has more tax advantages than any other investment. Real estate has tax deductions for the mortgage payments, depreciation of property, insurance, and maintenance costs. It offers tax-deferred growth, tax-free gains, tax-free withdrawals, stepped-up basis at death, and many other tax advantages. Compared with tax-advantaged retirement savings plans, real estate may provide a superior alternative for retirement funds, but with more risk.

Deposits into retirement savings plans are tax-deferred and taxed as ordinary income coming out, and taxable to beneficiaries of your estate. Investment real estate is tax-deferred with regard to capital gains and tax-free to beneficiaries because of what is called a "stepped-up cost basis," which occurs when the real estate is passed from your estate. Real estate is more liquid than a retirement plan and can more easily be coordinated with other asset purchases.

Say a person has $12,000 going into a pretax retirement savings plan. How many uses does his money have? Only one use. He cannot touch the money for any other reason without paying the taxes and incurring a penalty for early withdrawal, if he is less than 59½ years old. Earnings from the plan must remain inside the plan.

With $12,000 going into a mortgage to buy a rental property, the owner can use the rental income for other things, such as buying life insurance, funding a Roth IRA, or purchasing more investment real estate. There is more of a coordinated approach—more uses and more benefits. If you include life insurance in this mix of investments, at your death you have a death benefit; you also have a disability benefit, more tax deductions, more liquidity, better estate planning, and much more.

Your home and a rental property belong in your financial game plan. Without these two magnificent assets, your overall financial plan will be lacking. Add whole-life insurance to the picture and some tax-free municipal bonds and an RSP and you are beginning to build a fine orchestra of financial products that can be coordinated for significant results.

KEY POINTS
- A thirty-year mortgage may be more appropriate than a fifteen-year mortgage for most people.
- Cash is the most expensive way to purchase a home.
- Real estate has many tax advantages that no other investment can match.
- Real estate has high risk, time, and expense.
- Rental properties may be a good retirement alternative.

CHAPTER 12

The Road to Travel

For the most part, our society has done more good for more people than any other society in history. Many of us do not realize how fortunate we are. We sometimes take for granted that we have the right to do with our lives as we see fit. If we can get an education and then work hard, our capitalist system will reward us.

Given all that opportunity, it is up to each individual to protect his or her freedom, health, and financial well-being. We have many tools and information at our fingertips to perform well and achieve financial independence. However, we need to be careful of all the misinformation and inferior financial products in the marketplace.

How difficult is it to grow and protect our wealth in the twenty-first century? For those who do not yet have wealth, the road to wealth is clear, although not always easy to navigate. For those who have wealth, there is a constant need to manage, care for, and protect it.

If people simply and faithfully saved 15 percent of their monthly income and lived on 85 percent of their income, they would probably avoid any financial problems. But today most people save less than 3 percent of their income. Given an average inflation rate of 3 percent a year, it is no wonder that people struggle to get ahead.

To show how easy it can be to have wealth, if every person saved $100 a month from age 21 to age 65 and invested it into a relatively safe financial product, he or she would have over $1 million at age 65. Today, fewer than 1 percent of North Americans age 65 or older have amassed that much cash or other liquid assets.

Ironically, many people lose more than $100 a month—every month—and they often don't even know they are losing it. They overpay their income taxes by not taking advantage of legitimate ways to reduce taxes. They may pay out interest on expensive consumer loans and credit-card debt. They may structure their home mortgage in the wrong way and pay too much in monthly mortgage costs. They often have the wrong type of insurance, overpaying premiums or getting no return on their payments. They settle for low yields on savings. They do not protect themselves from losing money in the stock market and tie up their money in retirement savings plans that cause a stress in other aspects of their financial lives. We find all of these problems even before we analyze their unnecessary expenditures for miscellaneous consumer products that become obsolete or are never used.

Sure, part of our freedom is being able to buy and enjoy what we want. But people need to think of the consequences of their spending, and of their own and their family's financial well-being. Well over 50 percent of divorces today are directly related to money problems, according to many marriage counselors.

Our economy flourishes as the envy of the world. Yet so many of our citizens can't make ends meet. If you took away most people's Social Security checks, we would have millions of destitute elderly. What, then, is the problem? People have jobs that pay well, income opportunity, freedom of information, and aspirations for the good life. They seem to have it all but never fulfill their dreams. They resort to buying lottery tickets as their hope for financial security.

I have studied this problem for over thirty-five years and have discovered that people's inability to save has two components. The smaller component is a lack of personal discipline. But the far larger component is the general lack of financial or economic education and the misinformation in the media and financial literature.

To be sure, there is a "greed factor" when it comes to saving and investing. Everyone would like to become rich and do it quickly. That would certainly be nice, but the world we live in does not make getting rich that easy, at least not for the vast majority of people. The appeal to get rich quickly is always alive and well, and there is nothing wrong with "taking a chance" once in a while. But for all but a few, the foundation of financial well-being needs to be on a sound and solid base of savings and steady investments, and not on speculation and get-rich-quick schemes.

But the reason for financial failure can't be simply that people are greedy, or that they don't plan, or don't save. Even people who create financial plans and who do save often fail to establish any significant level of wealth. The problem is that people are not taught how to properly build wealth and protect it. They are also manipulated by the media and financial institutions to do what is expected.

There are few courses in primary or secondary school on the subject of personal financial economics. The few courses that exist, and the materials for those courses, are often sponsored or developed by financial institutions. I have witnessed large stock-brokerage firms giving seminars in the school systems for 9- and 10-year-old children.

Perhaps you've heard of the Latin phrase *caveat emptor,* which means "buyer, beware." Our society puts too much of a burden on consumers to figure everything out about personal finance. If you're looking for reliable resources for self-education in personal finance, you'll find slim pickings. Most are very weak when it comes to valuable content; often they're purely for advertising purposes or for selling their own financial products.

We are taught how to consume from an early age. But we are not taught the power of saving, investing, and building independent wealth. We are driven to the mega shopping malls by advertising, public relations, and product promotion. But we are never driven to put something away for our own financial well-being. We see designer clothing with labels that are supposed to impress. But no one would dare wear their bank account on their chest.

There is, however, a road to travel in order to get to the light at the end of the tunnel, or to the pot of gold at the end of the rainbow. That road needs to be studied by all consumers. I ask my clients: "If you do not have today what you want, or if you are financially frustrated, why would you not want to change the road you are on? Why ride with the masses? Why listen to the traditional vendors along that road?"

That road hasn't worked for millions of people for over 100 years. To be financially successful, you need to get off the road most traveled and get on the road to financial freedom and independence. You need a lifetime of planning, economic verification, and principles, all designed to accelerate your wealth through the use of a systematic and intelligent financial process.

Lifetime Economic Acceleration Process (LEAP)

Everyone should want to be on the road to financial freedom and success. But few take it. Let's define exactly what that road is, the LEAP to a better financial life.

LIFETIME

We are all born and we will all die. That we know. That is the only guarantee we have. Everything in between is uncertain.

But knowing that our lives are limited and finite, we must utilize the time we have to its fullest, to its maximum efficiency and effectiveness. Time is more precious than money. If time were a commodity, everybody would be saving money in order to buy more time.

We are all born with a thirty- to forty-year working life. During that period of time, we work and produce income. This is called "people at work." Then we retire, and we rely on what we have saved and invested. That is called "dollars at work."

Personal financial economics is nothing more than moving from people at work to dollars at work. You start with nothing. You work hard to produce dollars and put some away for when you are no longer working. In today's world, for those with good health, the retirement years can be as long as the working years were. Retirement can last thirty to forty years too. When you retire, the pile of money you have amassed allows you to live comfortably for the rest of your life. If you continue to manage your dollars at work successfully, and if you stay relatively healthy, you should have a happy and fruitful retirement phase of your life. Ultimately, you should have built a legacy for your children, grandchildren, or to those whom you believe perform good works on Earth.

It is simple—in theory. But this lifetime process of people at work and dollars at work has, in fact, been difficult for most people to manage. Unfortunately, time does not wait. Time wasted cannot be taken back. If you wait too long to start saving and investing, you may have to save too much each year in a shorter period of time in order to amass enough dollars at work to be sufficient for your retirement and lifetime aspirations.

In our financial lives, we are all born with only one opportunity to ride the exponential curve. There is only one accumulation phase, one growth phase, and one takeoff phase. If you start saving late and don't get to use the entire exponential curve, you can't choose which phase you lose.

Every year wasted, without saving and without investment, is a year lost on the back end of the curve—the takeoff phase—and that is where you find the real money and wealth. People at work should lead to money at work; and money at work is the goal.

Not only is there only one opportunity for you to ride the exponential curve, but even if you have a successful ride, there are eroding factors that will eat away at your pile of money. These eroding factors come from government, financial institutions, and corporations in the form of taxes, inflation, interest costs, market fluctuation, planned obsolescence, technological change, lawsuit, and investment fees and charges of various kinds. Some eroding factors we can see coming, but others we can't see until it is too late. These forces whittle away at our growing wealth whether we are rich, poor, or somewhere in the middle.

Your life should be like an ocean voyage, with you as the captain of the ship. You need to guide that ship of wealth to its destination through both calm and turbulent waters. Financial storms are always out there, but like a good captain, you should be prepared and have the necessary equipment and skill to get you through without the loss of life, limb, or money.

But too many people view themselves as mere passengers on the ship of life. Some allow others to captain their ships for them. Others ride ships without captains, adrift and out of control both in good times and when financial storms occur.

Saving money is the first key to a successful financial life voyage. Business owners know they have to make a profit each year to stay in business. The capital they have invested in their business must earn more than what they could get by simply investing the money in stocks or bonds, or they might as well close their business. Business owners try to get at least a 15 percent return on the capital they invest.

For individuals, it is often difficult to earn 15 percent on a consistent basis on savings and investments. Therefore, you must save 15 percent per year of your gross annual income in order to build a nest egg over time. Most people fail to become wealthy simply because they fail to save and invest 15 percent of their income into their own wealth-building personal financial "business."

In order to overcome the eroding factors, you need to set aside 15 percent of your income. This is because inflation is 3 percent or more, planned obsolescence takes another 3 percent, technological changes take another 3 percent, and then taxes take their large bite too. How can you stay ahead of the curve? You need to fight inflation, avoid taxes, lower living costs, and avoid unnecessary expenditures. Your money must grow efficiently and effectively over your lifetime. You must balance instant gratification against the long-term predictable costs of your needs and desires over your lifetime. Developing wealth is a lifelong process, one that takes understanding and a blend of offensive and defensive strategies. It is serious business.

ECONOMIC

Money should not be viewed as a game or points on a scoreboard. Money is a commodity and not a mathematical calculation. Money is only a coin, a piece of paper, or, in today's world, data processing—ink marks on a statement. Except as a collector's item, a coin or a piece of paper has no intrinsic value; money only has true value as a medium of exchange to purchase a product or a service. As I have stated in my seminars, or when I meet with a client, and as I have repeated in this book: "Money is not math, and math is not money."

Money can be taken away more easily than any other asset. Physical assets such as a painting, an antique car, jewelry, collectibles, artifacts, land, or a home must be stolen or sold for you to lose them. But this is not true of money. You can lose money legally, and you can lose a lot of it, without even knowing it.

Every day someone is figuring out new ways to get at your money through perfectly legal means. Corporations are thinking of how to make new products you will want to buy. Financial services firms are thinking of new ways they can get you to let them use your money—and pay them a fee to do it. And government officials are thinking of new ways they can tax your money and use it for public programs you may or may not believe are worthwhile.

We put locks on our doors, lock our cars, keep our jewelry in safe-deposit boxes, and install alarm systems in our homes. Yet we leave our money up for grabs, free to be taken. The old saying that "money is hard-earned but easy to lose" is very profound.

Even the financial planning that some people do will not solve their problems, because the basic theory behind traditional financial planning is not economic but mathematical. Financial planning treats money as math, and not as a commodity. Mathematical approaches ignore the realities of the world in which we live. There is no understanding of the characteristics of money and the ease with which it can be eroded.

What individuals need is not financial planning but a personal financial and economic system. This system must have a number of important characteristics.

1. It must be universally applicable; it must work under any financial circumstances.
2. It must be dynamic and flexible; it must adjust to changing circumstances and changes in assumptions.
3. It must be verifiable; you must be able to measure whether it is on course at any point in time.
4. It must take into account global economic and even political circumstances as well as personal economic circumstances.
5. It must be efficient and it must be inexpensive to maintain; gains in financial performance created by using the system should not be eaten up by the cost of professional advice to manage the system.
6. It must be easy to implement and put into practice.
7. Finally, and most importantly, it must be holistic; it must take into account all of the moving parts of an individual's or a family's personal economic situation. This holistic approach must be based on sound economic and financial principles.

Before I developed the LEAP system in 1980, no such system existed. Since that time, I have continuously refined the LEAP system and the model it is based on to enhance these characteristics.

The difference between LEAP and typical financial planning systems is that LEAP contains within it a rigorous and valid economic and financial model. Without a valid economic and financial model, a financial planner's recommendations and an individual's decisions are based on unproven concepts, bias, personal opinion, convenience, and sales persuasion. Without a valid model, it is impossible to verify plan results.

For a financial model to be valid, and to provide increased opportunity for wealth building and wealth protection, it must take into account all of the eroding factors that decrease the value of money over time. The model must contain strategies for overcoming those eroding factors or for recapturing their costly effects. The model must also take into account global economic forces, since they have an effect on individual household finances as well as on the finances of nations.

The model that governs LEAP is called the PS&G Model, which stands for Protection, Savings, and Growth. The PS&G Model provides individuals and families with the ability to develop a coherent, holistic approach to managing their financial lives. The PS&G Model contains within it every possible financial decision an individual can make, and shows how each financial decision works. Each decision is then integrated with every other asset, in order to make the individual's money work harder and better. The model allows an individual to see and understand every advantage and disadvantage of all of the different financial decisions he or she has to make. The key is to enhance the advantages while eliminating the disadvantages of each decision. This cannot be done without a financial model.

Instead of thinking of financial life as a set of discrete, point-in-time decisions, which is the way traditional "needs, goals, and objectives" financial planning operates, the PS&G Model allows you to see how all of your assets work together to form a cohesive holistic model that solves all of your financial needs and goals with all of your money working in concert together.

An analogy I often use to describe LEAP financial decision making is that of a symphony orchestra. If all the instruments start a piece of music on a different measure, they can all be keeping the same time but merely producing noise. If instruments are placed randomly on the stage, they can all be playing the same piece and starting on the same measure, but they will still produce only noise. To be in harmony, the musicians have to be placed in the right place onstage so the sound is balanced, they must start the piece of music at the same place, and they must play together.

The LEAP system—and the PS&G Model—allows you to place all of your assets in the one correct position and in proper balance to achieve a financial symphony rather than financial noise. **By putting together your financial assets at the right time, in the right order, and in the right place, you can meet all of your financial needs, goals, and objectives without ever having to make mathematical calculations or create bar charts, pie charts, or columns and columns of numbers, page after page. At any given time, every person has one optimum financial position in which his or her current assets could be placed to get to maximum effectiveness and efficiency.**

ACCELERATION

Acceleration is the key concept that differentiates LEAP from traditional planning approaches. Just as Newton stated that "objects at rest tend to stay at rest and objects in motion tend to stay in motion," the same is true for money. It's important to remember that analogy. Money at rest stays at rest and erodes, due to the ever-present eroding factors, while money in motion stays in motion and can be put to work multiple times to overcome the eroding factors.

The acceleration-of-money theory is very simple. **Assets that are kept in one financial instrument over time only attain one use or one benefit. They only earn one interest, or one dividend, or one capital gain, or one rental income, or one of some other form of earning. Whatever form that earning takes, the money earned is being lost to the eroding factors.** By moving earnings into other financial instruments in the right balance and at the right time, the effect is to increase your personal money supply. The result of money acceleration can be a substantial reduction in income taxes and financial fees or charges, or a lowering of premiums and other expenses. Money acceleration can also reduce the effects of inflation while increasing the overall rate of return on your money. By properly utilizing money acceleration, you can achieve a possible effective overall rate of return of 15 percent while adding no risk to your portfolio of financial instruments. Whether you reach 15 percent or not will depend on your income and your asset mix, but one thing is for sure: You will improve your returns over your current financial situation.

Figure 12.1 shows a few products that provide great opportunity for acceleration and a few products that provide little opportunity for acceleration.

Figure 12.1

CONTAIN ACCELERATION	LACK ACCELERATION
MONEY MARKET ACCOUNTS	RETIREMENT SAVINGS PLANS
MUTUAL FUNDS	ANNUITIES
WHOLE LIFE INSURANCE	TERM LIFE INSURANCE
REAL ESTATE	ZERO COUPON BONDS

Other financial products, such as certificates of deposit and individual stocks and bonds, provide a moderate opportunity for acceleration.

This discussion is by no means intended to label some products as inherently "good" and others as inherently "bad." To be sure, it is important to have some personal wealth in products that offer low opportunity for acceleration; tax-deferred retirement savings plans are a good case in point, which I discussed in detail in chapter 10. I am saying, however, that you should not be putting a disproportionate amount of your wealth into low-acceleration-opportunity financial products, as many people are these days. Once you do that, you are slowing down your wealth-growing potential and exposing yourself to the ravages of the eroding factors.

What acceleration does is add more "wealth potential" to an underlying financial instrument. Too often people project the amount of wealth that can be created over time merely by calculating the yield and disregarding potential. But sometimes low-yield products with high acceleration potential can add more wealth than a higher-yielding financial product without acceleration capabilities.

PROCESS

LEAP is a process. The PS&G Model allows for a systematic analysis of protection, savings, and growth decisions. Since the idea is to coordinate all of your money decisions into one efficient and effective system, you can participate in this financial construction project because of the hands-on PS&G Model. Like an architect, engineer, or doctor, you should base your financial life on a scientific and procedural method, not one based on haphazard choices from time to time that are not coordinated with one another. The LEAP system operates on the assumption that an individual and his or her LEAP advisor will consider global, national, and personal financial data in order to amend and redesign the program from time to time. The LEAP advisor acts as a "macro manager," working with you and your other advisors, such as an accountant or attorney, to produce a comprehensive, coherent, and holistic personal economic plan.

The Road to Financial Success

In summary, be serious and focused about putting your financial life in order. It will make your life less stressful and more enjoyable. **The key to a successful financial life is to have a solid base of financial products that are coordinated and integrated. They must include protection products, savings products, and investment products. By using the acceleration process instead of the accumulation process, you can**

achieve more benefits and money supply throughout your lifetime.

You should save at least 15 percent of your gross annual income each year and have at least six months of income in savings that are liquid and available at all times.

Maximize your insurance coverage to the amount that replaces the value of every item that you own, including your own life. Use term-life insurance only as a temporary way to cover your life insurance needs, but convert to whole-life permanent insurance as soon as possible.

Avoiding taxes is far better than just deferring them. Take every opportunity to minimize or eliminate taxes. Taxes are the largest eroding factor because they take money from you when you earn it, when you save it, when you invest it, when you withdraw it, and when you leave it to your heirs.

Avoid high-interest loans that are not tax-deductible. Use "other people's money" for college education and not your own. Avoid locking your money up into single-dimensional need-only accounts that are governed by rules and laws.

Retirement planning should be diversified with several sources of income, not just a qualified savings account. Since you may live a long time while not working, you need a powerful set of resources that provide income, stay ahead of inflation, and allow you to enjoy your money rather than locking it up.

Investments must be diversified as well—that means some stocks, some bonds, some mutual funds, some real estate, and a small business, as well as government securities.

Think of all your financial decisions as an orchestra positioned properly and in harmony. The key is to have a conductor to keep everything in balance. Your LEAP representative can assist you in following these financial principles and designing a financial model for you and your family that will increase your knowledge and understanding of your own financial potential.

Remember, money is not math and math is not money. Money is a commodity and it is constantly under assault from a multitude of eroding factors. You cannot predict the future. Money is hard-earned but easily lost. Stay in control of it. Protect it. Do not follow the crowd, since most of them are going down the road that is most often traveled and they will fail. As the title of Scott Peck's bestseller states, you must go down "the road less traveled" to succeed.

KEY POINTS

• Save at least 15 percent of your gross income each year.
• Have at least six months of your gross annual income in liquid savings.
• Maximize your insurance coverage to insure for the full replacement value of any asset lost, including your own life.
• Use the cash-flow-of-money system that moves money from one asset to another to gain a greater rate of return, more benefits, and tax savings. (This is the key to real wealth potential.)
• Have balance between protection, savings, and investments—diversification of assets, not just portfolios.
• Avoid or reduce taxes in every possible area of your life.
• Have whole-life insurance death benefits equal to your net worth at retirement.
• Have an exit strategy for your retirement savings plans to avoid being taxed when you need the money most.
• Understand lost-opportunity costs on taxes, fees, expenses, term insurance policies, interest charges, low-yield savings, and high-cost mortgages.
• Keep debt to a minimum by being on a cash basis except for home mortgages.

LIFETIME ECONOMIC ACCELERATION PROCESS
"We add value to life"